INSIDE STORIES FROM THE FORBIDDEN CITY

*Written by Er Si, Shang Hongkui
and Others*

Translated by Zhao Shuhan

NEW WORLD PRESS
BEIJING, CHINA

First Edition 1986

Cover Design by Sun Chengwu

ISBN 0-8351-1664-6

Published by
NEW WORLD PRESS
24 Baiwanzhuang Road, Beijing, China

Printed by
FOREIGN LANGUAGES PRINTING HOUSE
19 West Chegongzhuang Road, Beijing, China

Distributed by
CHINA INTERNATIONAL BOOK TRADING COR-
    PORATION (Guoji Shudian)
P.O. Box 399, Beijing, China

Printed in the People's Republic of China

CONTENTS

FOREWORD

This collection of stories describing events which took place in the imperial palace of the Ming (1368-1644) and Qing (1644-1911) dynasties is based on materials in the imperial archives of these two great dynasties.

The former imperial palace, located immediately behind the gate-tower of Tiananmen (Gate of Heavenly Peace) in the geographical centre of Beijing, served as the political headquarters for the administration of the empire as well as the living quarters of the imperial family. Popularly known as the Forbidden City, it accommodated a total of twenty-four feudal sovereigns over a span of some five hundred years, from the early fifteenth to the early twentieth century. Detailed records were kept of the daily life of the "Sons of Heaven", as well as of events occurring at court and in the inner palace, where the empresses and concubines lived. Although no common people had access to this vast corpus of written material, certain anecdotes and rumours concerning the inhabitants of the Forbidden City — from the emperors, imperial consorts and eunuchs down to palace maids — found their way out of the palace and spread through society at large. A large number of unofficial histories were produced describing these aspects of the feudal court.

The Forbidden City is no longer a "forbidden" place. It has been converted into a museum and many of its once veiled archives have been published in book form. The majority of the authors of the stories contained in this volume have personally examined the documents and dossiers of the Ming and Qing dynasties in an effort to make their contributions historically accurate.

For years, many different opinions have been raised regarding the cause of death of the Qing Emperor Tongzhi. To provide an authoritative answer to this question, Xu Yipu examined the "Records of Imperial Medical Prescriptions", from which he obtained detailed data on the pulse and physiopathological condition of the ailing emperor. From this he was able to conclude that Tongzhi died of smallpox rather than syphilis or scabies, as has been alleged by some historians.

Why the death of the succeeding Emperor Guangxu is even more problematical is due to his role in the complex political struggles of the late Qing era. Some say that Guangxu was poisoned to death by his political rival, the Empress Dowager Cixi, while others claim that the Northern warlord Yuan Shikai was responsible for the emperor's "sudden demise". Still others lay the blame on the Empress Dowager's trusted eunuch Li Lianying. After looking into the reform-minded emperor's case history, now preserved in the Palace Museum, and consulting medical experts, Zhu Jinfu, summed up his conclusions in "the True Cause of Emperor Guangxu's 'Sudden Death'".

Because it offers fresh evidence for the solution of a number of important historical questions, *Inside Stories from the Forbidden City* makes intriguing and worthwhile reading.

Qian Xinsheng

FIRES IN THE FORBIDDEN CITY

Er Si

Most ancient buildings in China were constructed of wood, which made them highly susceptible to fires. Given this risk, however, the greatest damage was caused if the structures were struck by lightning.

THE FIRST MAJOR "HEAVENLY FIRE"

When the Forbidden City, whose construction began in 1406 during the reign of the Ming Emperor Yongle, was completed in 1420, the Ming Dynasty moved its capital from Nanjing to Beijing. When Yongle held court in the Hall of Heavenly Mandate to celebrate the lunar New Year, the last thing he expected was that his throne hall would be struck by lightning four months later. Destroying the three most important palace halls (the Halls of Heavenly Mandate, Canopy and Prudence), the accident shook the entire empire and placed the "Son of Heaven" in a predicament: he had to issue an edict inviting criticism from his ministers. Zou Ji, an imperial censor, responded by submitting a "Memorial on the Fire in the Hall of Heavenly Mandate", in which he expressed concern about the huge amount of money that would have to go into its reconstruction, recalling that "thousands upon thousands of common people laboured for years to build it". Some court officials were so pessimistic that they proposed moving the imperial capital back to Nanjing. This enraged the emperor, who had one of them executed on the grounds that abandoning Nanjing as the capital was decided "through deliberation by all the ministers of the court". While indicating how much sincerity lay in Yongle's soliciting opinions from his subjects, this episode sheds some light on the enormous damage the 1421 conflagration inflicted on the Ming palace.

Reconstruction of the three halls was completed two decades later, that is, in late 1441, the sixth year of the Zhengtong reign.

THE SECOND CALAMITOUS FIRE

The year 1557, the 36th year of the Jiajing reign, witnessed a major fire in the Ming palace that "devoured the Halls of Heavenly Mandate, Canopy and Prudence" and spread as far as the Meridian Gate. These halls were not rebuilt until 1562.

Reputedly an illustrious sovereign, Emperor Jiajing ordered numerous construction projects to be carried out during his reign, including the Hall of the Supreme Master, the Thunder Terrace and other buildings for the practice of Taoism. But Jiajing's deities did little to prevent the 1557 conflagration which consumed the major portion of the outer palace, forcing him to attend to affairs of state in the Hall of Literary Glory rather than the destroyed Hall of Imperial Supremacy.

The amount of destruction this fire caused can be judged from the fact that the 30,000 labourers who were employed to clear the debris worked from three o'clock in the morning till seven in the evening and made use of 5,000 carts.

According to the Ming Dynasty *Book of Imperial Administration*, Emperor Jiajing decided to rebuild the Meridian Gate the same year the fire occurred. "To raise the necessary funds, the Boards of Revenue, War and Works were each to contribute 300,000 taels of silver. Censors were dispatched to collect funds to purchase building materials, which the various localities had to provide to the Board of Works. Provincial governors and judges were ordered to turn in all fines and the salaries for unfilled official positions. The various departments in the capital were to make inventories of the materials delivered by the provinces and hand them over to the central authorities for use on the project."

Moreover, huge numbers of soldiers and civilian workers were conscripted for the purpose. "Other projects were suspended and, as during the earlier construction of the Palace of Heavenly Purity, all soldiers who could be conveniently released from military service and the Brocade Uniform Imperial Guards were used to rebuild the Meridian Gate." Zhili (now Hebei) and Henan provinces also supplied an enormous labour force.

The construction of palace buildings during the Jiajing reign was a crushing burden on the common people. Recurrent taxation and corvée labour forced many commoners to flee from their homes. Censor Liu Kui submitted a memorial to the throne on this situation (having bought a coffin beforehand in case his confrontation with the emperor led to his being beheaded): "How much money remains in the imperial treasury? How much can be collected every year? Now that a single project costs hundreds of millions of taels of silver, the carpenters, masons and other craftsmen have become rich or secured official positions, while Taoist priests get preferential treatment from the imperial court. As a result, the state coffers are being depleted and the resources of the people are being exhausted. . . ." As had been expected, the emperor turned a deaf ear to Liu's warning and had him caned at court and imprisoned.

Another memorial submitted after the construction project was under way by a high official named Zhang Hanqing was more frank about the situation: "Now financial deficit is commonplace. This, combined with successive droughts and floods, has drained the material resources of the empire. . . . Liang Dong, supervisor of engineering, has reported that more money is needed. He intends to use the silver reserves of the Board of Revenue. . . . Money is first taken from the imperial household, then from the Board of Revenue, and then from the local people; but the last named have no one to turn to. There has been so much famine in the southeastern part of the empire that peasants have been forced to eat each other's flesh. . . ."

Embezzlement was rife in the course of building palace halls. Yan Song (1480-1567), tutor to the heir-apparent (actually the prime minister), helped himself to so much public money that his holdings exceeded those of the imperial treasury. He sold official titles and the recipients in turn bribed him with some of the money they obtained by dipping into the public purse. Yan's main flunkey, Zhao Wenhua (?-1557), Vice-Minister of the Board of Works, used the building materials and labourers originally earmarked for the palace halls to build a private residence.

"Numerous common people have died in poverty, while those struggling in the grip of starvation groan piteously. All this is beyond the knowledge of His Majesty." This quotation from a memorial to the emperor bespeaks the nationwide consequence of the palace fire of 1557.

THE THIRD CONFLAGRATION

Again regarded as the "work of Heaven", another fire broke out in 1597, the 25th year of the Wanli reign. The three main halls of the Forbidden City burned down a third time, and the two principal buildings in the living quarters of the imperial family — the Palace of Heavenly Purity and the Palace of Earthly Tranquillity — were also destroyed. The fire took place at a time when the Ming house was in decline, and the reconstruction of these buildings took more than three decades to complete.

Once again the whole nation suffered. In the chapter "Production and Commerce" in the *History of the Ming Dynasty* it is written, "To restore the three palace halls, officials toured Hubei, Hunan, Sichuan and Guizhou provinces to procure such precious timber as *nanmu* (*phoebe nanmu*) and China fir. Obtaining this wood involved an expenditure of upwards of 9.3 million taels of silver."

One episode in the rebuilding of the Palace of Heavenly Purity and the Palace of Earthly Tranquillity illustrates the degree of corruption in the Ming court. When 900,000 taels of silver remained after the completion of the project, He Shengrui, a senior secretary in the Board of Works in charge of the reconstruction, chose not to comply with the current practice of bribing the eunuchs and dividing the money among his colleagues, but rather turned it over to the state treasury instead. Little did he expect that this would result in his being demoted on the charge of inflating engineering costs. He Shengrui defended himself by submitting to the throne an impassioned memorial which was turned down. When the honest official died, his son He Zhongshi wrote an essay entitled "An Orphan Appeals to Heaven", in which he recounts in detail his father's activities in connection with the reconstruction of the palace buildings. Given the circumstances of the time, it is not hard to imagine what young He's efforts amounted to.

In addition to the three "heavenly fires" described above, there was another notable fire attributable to human factors. This occurred at the Lantern Festival in 1514, the ninth year of the reign of Emperor Zhengde. The Lantern Festival takes place two weeks after the lunar New Year, a time when the whole palace was immersed in merry-making. The fire began when a defective silk lantern set a carpet on fire, and the eventual conflagration reduced the Palace of Heavenly Purity and the Palace of Earthly Tranquillity to ashes.

During the Qing Dynasty, the only major fire in the

palace took place in 1888, the 14th year of the Guangxu reign. In this blaze the gates of Virtuous Government, Supreme Harmony and Manifest Virtue and the nearby storerooms were destroyed. A fire caused by lightning broke the following year and laid waste to the Hall of Prayers for Good Harvest in the Temple of Heaven. As the structure was made of fine *nanmu* wood, people living kilometres away were able to smell the fragrant smoke it gave off as it burned. The building was restored to its present splendour in the following year.

The Forbidden City experienced an instance of arson in 1923 after the 1911 Republican Revolution which overthrew the Qing Dynasty. The abdicated emperor, Aisin-Gioro Puyi, who was still living in the Inner Palace at the time, requested that an inventory be taken of the former imperial warehouses because his huge family was running into mounting economic difficulties. On the night of June 26, the West Palace was consumed by flames which destroyed most of the buildings in the garden of the Palace of Felicity together with the valuable historical and cultural relics stored there. In his book *From Emperor to Citizen*, Puyi described the accident as arson perpetrated by eunuchs attempting to destroy evidence of their theft of palace treasures.

THE SOUTH PALACE COUP AND EMPEROR JINGTAI'S DEATH

Wang Tianyou

The Ming Dynasty suffered chronically from intense power struggles among members of the imperial household. The South Palace Coup in the middle period of the dynasty, which led to the death of Emperor Jingtai (reigned 1450-1456), furnishes a classic example.

The coup was engineered by Emperor Yingzong, who first reigned between 1436 and 1449, the year in which he was taken prisoner while leading a military expedition against a Mongolian tribe, led by Yexian (1407-1454). During his absence, his half brother Prince Chengwang attended to state affairs as Lord Protector but then assumed the title of Emperor Jingtai. Relying on competent generals and ministers, the new sovereign strengthened border defences and carried out political reforms which revitalized the dynasty.

The Yexian tribe was defeated by the Minister of War Yu Qian (1398-1457), who proposed to Emperor Jingtai that Yingzong be welcomed back to the capital. But his proposal was not accepted by the self-ish Emperor Jingtai until the general had submitted repeated memorials on the necessity of considering the overall interests of the country. On his return from the territory occupied by Yexian, Emperor Yingzong was accommodated in the South Palace outside the Forbidden City. He was placed under house arrest with only a few attendants at his side. He was even restricted in his use of stationery for fear that he would contact outsiders and carry out a conspiracy.

In the third year of his reign, Emperor Jingtai made one of his own sons heir-apparent. This was a direct threat to Emperor Yingzong's eldest son, who was then made Prince Yi. Soon afterwards, Yingzong was accused of "plotting to reinstate his son's heirship and seeking help outside the palace by presenting a sword to a follower". Actually, Yingzong made a gift of a sword to Ruan Lang, his personal attendant, who in turn gave it to Wang Yao, a student of Ruan's who was serving as a security officer in the imperial palace. The suspicious Emperor Jingtai had Ruan and Wang executed and sought to punish Yingzong. He took no further retaliatory measures only because of the patient advice of some unbiased court officials.

Quite unexpectedly, the new heir-apparent died of an illness in the winter of the fourth year of Jingtai's reign. His premature death intensified the struggle taking place around the question of restoring the heirship to Emperor Yingzong's son. Senior Secretary Zhang Lun of the Board of Rites, Imperial Censor Zhong Tong and a number of others were flogged in the presence of Emperor Jingtai for having openly discussed reinstating the deposed heir-apparent. Zhong was beaten so severely that he died shortly afterwards. Two years later, Xu Zheng, a supervisory official in the Board of Punishments, suggested that Yingzong and his eldest son Prince Yi be moved to Yizhou, the son's ostensible fiefdom. This proposal naturally upset the former emperor. When Emperor Jingtai fell ill early in the eighth year of his reign, more ministers began calling for Prince Yiwang's reinstatement, though without success. But events developed so rapidly that a coup took place one night, leading to Yingzhong's restoration the next morning.

The plan for the coup was worked out in two top-secret meetings whose participants included Cao Jixiang, a eunuch in charge of the Beijing garrison forces; Xu Youzhen, an associate censor; General Shi Heng; and Zhang Ni and Zhang Yue, both military governors. Early in the evening, Shi planted more than 1,000 of his soldiers in the imperial palace while Xu and the others accompanied Yingzong to the palace gate. When the guards tried to stop them from entering, the former sovereign shouted, "Don't you know I am the emperor?" and other guards who offered resistance were berated by him. Thus the party entered the Forbidden City almost unobstructed, and the next morning Yingzong held court and declared his resumption of the throne.

In his edict on his restoration, Emperor Yingzong condemned Jingtai for having usurped power. Then, in the name of the Empress Dowager, he listed his rival's crimes: arrogating the Mandate of Heaven, imprisoning a real emperor, illegally making his own son heir-apparent, breaking with ancestral customs and disobeying state laws, wallowing in luxury, and placing his trust in wicked officials. "He has violated the principles of filial piety," Yingzong went on, "brotherly love, benevolence and righteousness. His immoral actions have aroused the indignation of both the gods and all mankind." In this way, the re-enthroned ruler expressed grievances that had been pent up inside him for the past seven years.

Jingtai retained the title of Prince Chengwang and went to live in the West Inner Palace, and within one month, he fully recovered from his illness. At this time, Emperor Yingzong ordered a trusted eunuch, Jiang An, to strangle Jingtai to death, and his corpse was buried in the Western Hills outside Beijing, rather than in the Ming Tombs, now a scenic sight in Beijing. The tomb of his empress, who had died some years earlier, was destroyed, and his favourite concubines were given cords with which to hang themselves. The only exception was Imperial Concubine Wang, who fell into disgrace with Jingtai for having disapproved of his depriving Yingzong's eldest son of his heirship.

Others implicated in the struggle for supreme power were Jingtai's former loyal eunuchs and ministers, including Minister Yu Qian, who was executed on Yingzong's order. All reform measures begun in the Jingtai reign were abolished. These actions, plus Yingzong's indiscriminate promotion and rewarding of those who aided him in his restoration, heralded yet another period of power struggles by careerist eunuchs and self-centred partisans, which further undermined the stability of the dynasty.

In their treatment of Yingzong's South Palace coup and Jingtai's death, many Ming historians made efforts to evade the facts. *The Veritable Records of Emperor*

Yingzong contains profuse details about Jingtai's illness and suggests that he died a natural death. *A Daily Record of Emperor Yingzong's Tianshun Reign Period* (1457-1464), *A Record of Restoration* and *A Record of Storming the Palace Gate* say nothing in particular about Jingtai's end. Lu Yi, in his *Random Notes Taken During Illness*, was somewhat more objective: "Emperor Jingtai died of strangulation with a silk cord at the hand of the eunuch Jiang An."

Scholars of the Qing Dynasty were somewhat more straightforward in discussing this event, and there was a tendency to be more critical of Yingzong than of Jingtai. In 1769, the 34th year of his reign, the Qing Emperor Qianlong had a stone tablet erected in Jingtai's honour with an inscription as follows: "Emperor Jingtai cannot be said to have rendered no outstanding services to the empire if one remembers his ordering Yu Qian to fight the border tribes against the objections of many other court officials. His selfishness became clear when he had Yingzong detained in the South Palace on the latter's return to Beijing, and when he made his own son heir-apparent. But Heaven dictated that Jingtai's son should die. Later, Jingtai was killed and buried in the Western Hills, for which the emperor had only himself to blame. On the other hand, can Emperor Yingzong escape being ridiculed for his ingratitude and shallowness of mind?"

AN EMPEROR BORN IN THE "COLD PALACE"

Er Si

Many strange things occurred in the imperial palace during the Ming Dynasty (1368-1644) due to the fact that most of the sovereigns after Emperor Yongle (reigned 1403-1424) were either of low intelligence or incompetent. One of these was Emperor Chenghua (reigned 1465-1487). When he was a child, Chenghua's grandmother appointed a court lady named Wan to look after him. She took care of everything for the boy, from eating and playing to sleeping. Chenghua ascended the throne at the age of 16, when Wan was 35. Because of her intimate associations with the young emperor, she had a firm control over him and became one of his concubines despite the fact she was nineteen years his senior.

The first thing Wan did after becoming an imperial consort was to slander Empress Wu, Chenghua's favourite, before the emperor in the hope of consigning her to limbo. Swayed by his former nurse, Chenghua had Wu beaten for no good reason and then banished her to what was known as the "cold palace", a section of the imperial palace where disfavoured women lived. Wan's next plan was to bear the emperor a son, which would significantly elevate her position to that of queen mother, thereby placing both the reigning emperor and heir-apparent in the palm of her hand. *The History of the Ming Dynasty* says of her: "She was intelligent and sharp-witted and knew how to curry favour with the throne. She succeeded in deposing Empress Wu so that she could influence the emperor as no others could. Each time His Majesty was out on an inspection or sight-seeing tour, she would appear in his entourage, stunningly dressed in martial attire. . . . In the first month of the second year of the Chenghua reign, she gave birth to the first prince, which delighted the throne immeasurably. . . . She was then elevated to the position of imperial concubine of the first rank."

Wan's good fortune was short-lived, however. The first prince died soon after birth and she never became pregnant again. Out of jealousy, Wan saw to it that all the other pregnant imperial consorts were forced to have abortion, and in certain cases disposed of altogether.

As a result of her machinations, Emperor Chenghua was childless when he reached middle age. This naturally was a matter of great concern to the imperial household and the court as a whole. High officials, including Grand Secretary Peng Shi and Minister Yao Kui, presented memorials to the throne advising His Majesty to free himself of Imperial Concubine Wan's control. The emperor, however, was too weak-minded to act independently. At the same time, Wan went a step further in colluding with eunuchs such as Qian Neng, Qin Qin, Wang Zhi and Liang Fang, who had wormed their way to His Majesty's favour, as well as with her domineering relatives, such as Wan An. Together they formed a powerful clique which held sway over the court.

It was under these circumstances that a maid of honour became pregnant.

A PRINCE IN HIDING

In the early part of the Ming Dynasty, numerous punitive campaigns were launched against the border tribes, regarded by the court as "barbarians". The Chenghua reign was no exception. In one such campaign, the headman of a Guangxi tribe, named Ji, was killed, and his beautiful daughter was carried off to the imperial capital in Beijing. Because she was clever and a quick learner, in due course she became a court librarian. One day Emperor Chenghua met this Guangxi girl while he was strolling in the palace grounds. At that point, "His Majesty spent a night in her bedroom, after which she became with child".

The news of this event enraged Imperial Concubine Wan, who ordered one of her maids to force the pregnant Ji to abort the fetus. Little did Wan know that her maid was sympathetic to the young woman's plight and reported back that Ji had "a growth in her abdomen". Doubting the truth of this, Wan had Ji imprisoned in the Hall of Tranquillity and Happiness, which, despite its eloquent name, was actually the "cold palace".

When Ji gave birth to an infant boy, she asked a eunuch, Zhang Min, to drown the child, since she was

21

afraid of what would happen should Wan learn of the event. Zhang asked her in surprise, "How can we put the heir-apparent to death when His Majesty has been waiting for his arrival all these years?" Zhang purchased a supply of nutritious baby food and secretly asked a woman who lived outside the palace to take care of the baby. Wan, who later got wind of the birth, searched for the new-born prince, but in vain. The persecuted Empress Wu, who lived in the same place as Ji, learned what had happened and helped in the rearing of the unlucky boy. Six years elapsed without the throne knowing anything about the matter.

IMPERIAL JOY

One day Zhang Min was helping Emperor Chenghua comb his hair. "What a pity that I haven't got a son even at this advanced age," the sovereign murmured to himself. "Your subject deserves to die for not having reported that Your Majesty has had a son for many years," said the eunuch, prostrating himself on the ground. He then told the emperor the whole story of the prince in hiding. This came as a great surprise to Chenghua, who lost no time in arranging to see Court Lady Ji and having the prince escorted back to the imperial family.

A dramatic scene took place in the "cold palace". Standing before the imperial attendants who had come for the prince, Ji held her son in her arms, and said tearfully, "I will certainly die once you leave me." She dressed him in a vermilion robe. "My darling, they are going to present you to your father. He is a bearded old man in yellow robe," she told the boy.

According to *The History of the Ming Dynasty*, at this time the little boy's hair was long enough to touch the ground, for since his birth he had never once had a haircut. He was carried to the emperor in a sedan chair, and threw himself into his father's arms. His Majesty sat him on his knees and sized him up for quite a while before saying, tears streaming down his wrinkled cheeks, "Yes, you are my son. There is a definite resemblance." He then had his chief eunuch announce the great event to the whole court. "All the court officials were elated when they learned the good news. . . . The next day, they sought audience with His Majesty to extend their congratulations. An imperial decree followed, informing the whole empire of this occasion for universal joy." Court Lady Ji was granted the title of "Virtuous Imperial Concubine", and she moved into the Palace of Eternal Life in the Forbidden City.

In the festive atmosphere that enveloped the imperial palace, only Imperial Concubine Wan found no cause to celebrate. "I've been cheated by that pack of villains," she was often heard cursing.

Soon afterwards, a strange event transpired within the walls of the Forbidden City: the sudden death of Imperial Concubine Ji. *The History of the Ming Dynasty* comments: "Some said Imperial Concubine Wan put her to death. Others say Imperial Concubine Ji hanged herself." Even stranger, at this time the eunuch Zhang Min killed himself by swallowing gold.

The young prince was named Zhu Youcheng and was made the official heir-apparent. He was still in danger, however, since his mother was no longer alive to protect him. His grandmother, the Empress Dowager, stepped in and offered to take care of him, ensuring greater safety for the child. Unreconciled to her discomfiture, Wan continued scheme to snuff him out, and invited him to dine with her. Before going to Wan's palace, the vigilant Empress Dowager cautioned him not to eat anything there. Consequently, when the vicious concubine asked him to help himself to the delicacies on the table, the little boy said, "No, this food may be poisoned." "Even a mere child suspects me," Wan said to herself. "I'll die at his hand some day." After the banquet that night, Wan fell sick, never to recover.

Some years later, Youcheng ascended the throne as Emperor Hongzhi and ruled for the 18 years between 1488 and 1505.

A JUNIOR EUNUCH REMONSTRATES WITH HIS EMPEROR BY FEIGNING MADNESS

Feng Erkang

Chinese history is filled with famous stories of ministers successfully remonstrating with their sovereigns. Among the best-known were Zou Ji, Prime Minister of the state of Qi during the Warring States Period (475-221 B.C.), who boldly criticized King Weiwang on several occasions; and Wei Zheng, a high court official of the Tang Dynasty (618-907), who was said to have admonished Emperor Taizong on more than 200 major issues. However, rare is it that a eunuch, let alone a eunuch of junior rank, would dare to act in this manner. Though the episodes related here about the Ming Dynasty eunuch Achou, are not recorded in the official histories, they suggest the intelligence and resourcefulness of the rank and file in the imperial palace.

Achou (literally "Lovely Clown"), whose real name is unknown, served in the court of Emperor Chenghua (reigned 1465-1487) as a jester. One day, he and a number of other attendants were entertaining the emperor by playing drunk. "The Prime Minister is coming," someone said to him, cautioning him to behave himself in the presence of His Majesty. Achou turned a deaf ear to his colleague and continued his performance. "His Majesty's coming," his colleague added, but to no avail. "Eunuch Wang Zhi is here," came the third warning. Sobered by this last announcement, Achou put down his cup and adjusted his robe, preparing himself to greet Wang. "Why are you so afraid of Wang but don't care whether His Majesty is present?" asked another colleague. "You know," answered the jester, "eunuch Wang is too powerful for me to ignore."

Wang Zhi, head of a secret-special-service organization in the Ming court, abused his power and persecuted officials and common people to the extent that "merchants, travelling professionals, soldiers or other commoners could engage in their trades in peace". Grand Secretary Shang Lu (1414-1486) and other leading official of the day presented memorials to Emperor Chenghua calling for Wang's organization to be abolished. His Majesty, however, refused to listen and countered, "Why shouldn't the court use Wang Zhi to deal with evildoers?" He also tried to punish the leading memorialist. Achou, whose lowly position barred him from remonstrating directly with the emperor, feigned drunkenness as a means of suggesting to his sovereign that Wang was feared by even an intoxicated habitual drinker. It was clear that the old eunuch was a thorough tyrant. And Achou was politically-minded enough to worry that Wang might succeed in usurping supreme power.

In his disruptive activities, Wang Zhi was aided by imperial censors Wang Yue and Chen Yue. With these and a number of other flunkeys in his service, Wang consolidated and extended his position both inside and outside the court. To expose the crimes of the powerful eunuch's clique, Achou once played the role of a general swaggering across the street, a halberd (in Chinese, a halberd is called a *yue*) in each hand. When somebody asked him, "What's the purpose of those two halberds?" he replied, "They're my most powerful weapons in fighting the enemy. They've each got names: one is called Wang Yue, the other Chen Yue."

Fortunately, the throne was wise enough to know what his junior eunuch was hinting at. Achou's circumlocutory remonstration plus the advice of several of his ministers prompted Emperor Chenghua to banish Wang Zhi to a post far away from the imperial capital.

In a well-known historical episode, in the last years of the 3rd century B.C., Xiang Yu, the king of Chu, led 8,000 troops in a battle against his rival Liu Bang later the founder and first emperor of Han Dynasty (206 B.C.-220 A.D.). Soon afterwards, Xiang's troops deserted him when Liu made use of a ruse to demoralize them. When retelling this tale to Emperor Chenghua, Achou insisted that the king of Chu had only 6,000 troops. Asked why he had altered a historical fact, he replied, "Don't you know the other 2,000 have gone to build a mansion for Zhu Yong, the Duke of Baoguo?" Zhu Yong was a Ming general who was later appointed garrison commander of the capital. Utilizing his high position, he had his soldiers build a lavish residence for him. Achou's performance alerted the emperor to Zhu's action, which was soon cut short following an investigation ordered by the throne.

Since he was a habitual stammerer, Emperor Chenghua had difficulty discussing state affairs with his ministers or replying orally to their memorials. Consequently, Shi Chun, head of the Department of State Ceremonials, suggested that His Majesty "act according to conventional rules" in all cases. Pleased by this, the emperor promoted Shi to the rank of Minister of Rites. Achou, disgusted with the ridiculous way Chenghua employed his officials, once gave a performance before the emperor in which a stupid minister was shown appointing his subordinates. Playing the leading role in this satirical skit, Achou asked one of his "subordinates" what his name was. "I am Gong Lun (literally 'Public Opinion')." "Oh, you're useless," Achou said. "Who cares whether you are Gong Lun or not?" When another subordinate said his name was Gong Dao (literally "Impartiality"), Achou remarked, "Gong Dao? You're also out of date." A third man announced himself as Hu Tu (literally "Muddle-Headed"). "You are most welcome here," Achou said aloud, pleased that he had at long last found the right candidate.

PALACE MAIDS ATTEMPT TO STRANGLE EMPEROR JIAJING

Shang Hongkui

It may seem unbelievable, but a dozen young palace maids attempted to strangle the Ming Emperor Jiajing (reigned 1522-1566) with a silk cord. That he survived this assault was due to the fact that, in their hurry, the murderesses tied immovable knot in the cord rather than making a proper noose.

The case took place one night in 1452, the 21st year of the reign of Emperor Jiajing. According to *The History of the Ming Dynasty*, "His Majesty, who had been in poor health, spent the night in the palace of Imperial Concubine Duan. After he had fallen asleep, the palace maid Yang Jinying and a number of other maids collaborated to strangle him by tying a cord around his neck. They failed in their attempt, however, because they tied a fast knot. Zhang Jinlian, one of the maids on the scene, immediately reported the case to the empress, who rushed to the emperor's rescue and untied the knot. He was soon revived." *The Annals of the Ming Dynasty* contains roughly the same account and lists the nine palace maids who took part in the attempted murder.

Yang Jinying's confession is found in the Ming Dynasty archives: After nightfall, Imperial Concubines Wang and Cao approached Yang in the east anteroom of the inner palace and said, "Let's do it. In any case, it's better than dying at his hands." Yang Yuxiang prepared a silk cord and Yang Jinhua made a noose with it. As they approached the sleeping emperor, Yang Cuiying told Yao Shugao to seize him by the throat and said, "Pull it more tightly." They covered his face with a piece of yellow fabric, and Xing Cuilian pressed hand on his chest. Su Chuanyao held his left hand, and Guan Xiumei held his right. Liu Miaolian and Chen Juhua pinned his legs down while Yao and Guan yanked on the noose. But it was ineffective. When Empress Fang learned what had happened, she hurried to the scene and had the maids arrested.

The above description is found in a memorial to the throne submitted by the Board of Punishments. But it distorted the facts regarding Imperial Concubine Cao, who according to another official record had nothing to do with the case. Actually, because she was a favourite of the emperor, Cao was framed by the jealous Empress Fang as the chief instigator. Shortly after this, Cao, another imperial concubine named Wang and all the serving maids involved in the attempt were put to death by dismemberment. Capital punishment, which was said to be decreed by Emperor Jiajing, was actually proposed by Empress Fang, since at the time the emperor was so weak and frightened that he was incapable of thinking straight.

Jiajing's illness worsened as a result of this affair, but

no imperial physician dared prescribe any medicine because of the awesomeness of the responsibility. But the chief physician, Xu Shen, felt duty-bound to do something, and ventured to prescribe a large dose of a number of powerful substances. Some eight hours after taking the remedy, Jiajing coughed violently and spit up several litres of dark-coloured blood, whereupon he regained enough strength to speak. Xu was generously awarded for having saved the emperor, but not long afterwards the imperial physician fell seriously ill himself. "I was in a state of great agitation when treating the emperor after the attempted murder, knowing full well I would be executed should the prescription prove ineffective. This is why I myself have fallen ill, and there appears to be no cure."

When he learned that his favourite concubine Cao had been wronged, Emperor Jiajing grew increasingly uneasy, and voiced his suspicions that the palace was haunted by spirits. He asked his minister Xu Jie, "Has someone been wronged in connection with the attempt on my life? For several days, I feel I have been haunted by ghosts." Xu replied, "She was near to you in her lifetime. But she was executed for no good reason. She could certainly come and haunt Your Majesty." By "she" Xu Jie meant Imperial Concubine Cao.

What was the motive behind this extraordinary murder attempt? From Yang Jinying's confession, "In any case, it's better than dying at his hands", we may assume that the palace maids' lives were seriously threatened, and thus they were defending themselves by striking first. The author surmises that the cause of their action is related to Emperor Jiajing's obsession with making immortality pills which required the sacrifice of human lives. Quite possibly, the young maids in question were on a future list of "ingredients".

Historical records suggest that Jiajing was one of the most egotistical emperors in Chinese history. He had been the prince of a feudal state before his ascension to the throne in 1522. Having become the "Son of Heaven", he gave his father the posthumous title of emperor and moved the old man's remains to the imperial burial grounds in the Hills of Heavenly Longevity (the present-day Ming Tombs) 50 kilometres to the northwest of Beijing. Many of the court ministers objected to these acts, but they could do very little to change his mind. Jiajing then ordered the construction of his own mausoleum, the Yongling, in the Ming Tombs area. The huge project took four years to complete, during which time he made eleven inspection tours of the work in progress. Paradoxically, following the completion of his final resting place, Jiajing devoted most of his time to making the so-called pills of immortality in the West Garden of the palace. His obsessions with longevity and death coexisted in him in an almost comical fashion. It is clear, however, that Jiajing wanted to enjoy himself to the greatest extent possible — in his remaining years and in his afterlife as well.

There were, of course, more enlightened officials who remonstrated with Emperor Jiajing concerning his search for longevity. But few prevailed over this stupid ruler whose first concern was to extend his life. When, in the 19th year of his reign, the emperor enlisted the services of the alchemist Duan Chaoyong, a court official named Yang Zui advised the throne to think twice. For all his loyalty, he was given so many strokes of the bamboo that he never recovered.

The palace maids' unsuccessful attempt at Jiajing's life failed to arouse him from his obsession. As one record of Ming court life put it, "Since His Majesty moved into the West Inner Palace, he became so obsessed with making longevity pills that he began to neglect visiting the ancestral temple and praying for good harvests, to stop holding court regularly, and to estrange himself from his ministers." In his *Tales Picked Up at Random*, the Ming scholar Shen De wrote, "In the middle years of the Jiajing reign, the emperor took longevity pills which, it was said, proved effective. In the winter of the 31st year, the throne ordered the selection, from Beijing and elsewhere, of 300 girls between the ages of eight and 14 to be brought into the imperial palace. Again, in the 34th year, another 160 girls under the age of ten were drafted. The emperor did this on the advice of Tao Zhongwen (a Taoist and alchemist) who required the girls for the making of longevity pills."

This last quotation suggests the number of girls sacrificed for Jiajing's sake. That no further attempts on his life were reported was because, first, stricter security measures were taken and, second, the girls brought into the palace were too young to offer him any resistance.

A QUEEN MOTHER IMPRISONED FOR TWENTY YEARS

Xu Qixian

The world-renowned Ming Tombs is the burial site of thirteen of the sixteen Ming Dynasty emperors. The tomb of Emperor Wanli (reigned 1573-1619) and his two empresses, known as the Dingling, is one of the largest and most interesting in the entire complex. Tucked away in a picturesque corner, the Dingling is composed of a magnificent Spirit Tower and an underground palace, where a large number of precious burial objects were found. The visitor will naturally think that all members of the imperial family must have enjoyed a life of incomparable wealth and splendour. This is not necessarily true, for Empress Xiaojing, entombed beside Emperor Wanli, had her cup of misery filled many times during her lifetime.

Empress Xiaojing was the posthumous title of Imperial Concubine Wang, originally a maid of honour serving Emperor Wanli's mother, Empress Dowager Cisheng. Wang's good looks attracted Wanli, and before long she became pregnant. When his mother asked him about this matter, Wanli at first denied having anything to do with the palace maid. But he had forgotten that there was in the court an imperial official whose duty was to record the daily activities of the emperor in great detail. The Empress Dowager produced *The Records of the Everyday Life of His Imperial Majesty*, which disarmed her son. Thereupon she said, "I'm an old woman, and I have no grandson. It would be considered good fortune for our whole imperial household if Wang could bear you a son. Despite her lowly status, she deserves to be promoted to the rank of imperial concubine." In the eighth month of tenth year of the Wanli reign (1582), that is, four months after she became an imperial concubine, the beautiful lady gave birth to a boy infant, Zhu Changluo, who was to have the briefest reign of the Ming empire as Emperor Taichang for only 29 days. As a matter of course, she could expect to receive all the honours due a queen mother. Awaiting her, however, was a life of utter wretchedness.

Though it was nothing unusual for a feudal emperor to consort with a maid of honour, it was not necessarily considered a credit to the ruler from the ethical point of view. Moreover, since Emperor Wanli made Wang an imperial concubine at his mother's urging, he regarded this as a loss of face which sowed seeds of discord between him and the unlucky lady. It was around this time that another court lady, Zheng, was made an imperial concubine. Being pretty and clever and knowing how to please the emperor and befriend those around her, Zheng quickly worked herself into His Majesty's good graces and became a natural rival of

Wang. Zheng's position was significantly elevated when she bore Wanli a son in the 14th year of his reign. The struggle now centred around the question of which boy was to be declared heir-apparent.

Soon after Zheng gave birth to a son, Wanli gave the woman the title of "Imperial Concubine of the First Rank", implying that her son was to be proclaimed heir-apparent. This move clearly put Wang in a less favourable position. According to feudal dynastic practice, the selection of the heir to the throne was a matter of first importance requiring the approval of the Empress Dowager and the support of the court ministers. This complicated the struggle, which was to last for 15 years. Jiang Yinglin, a supervising official in the Board of Revenue, was the first to memorialize the throne and suggest that His Majesty change his mind and proclaim Lady Wang "Imperial Concubine of the First Rank". Since the boy was the eldest prince, Jiang argued, he should naturally be entitled to succeed the throne. "Otherwise," Jiang stressed, "it would contradict traditional ethics, make the people's hearts and minds uneasy, and set a bad example for posterity." Another official, Sun Rufa of the Board of Punishments, said in a memorial to the sovereign, "Lady Zheng was made Imperial Concubine of the First Rank soon after the birth of her son, while Lady Wang received no promotion even five years after giving birth to the eldest prince. People cannot but suspect His Majesty's partiality to one side at the other's expense."

Memorials of this kind angered the emperor, for he considered them too incriminating. He therefore had both Jiang and Sun demoted to the rank of junior county officials. Other officials within the imperial cabinet also advised the throne to abide by tradition in determining who should be the emperor's rightful successor. Wanli not only refused to listen as before, but also had some of these officials reprimanded, caned, removed from office, demoted, sent back to their home villages, or even thrown into prison. Wang herself was consigned to the "cold palace" as a virtual prisoner.

In the 29th year of Wanli's reign, Wang's son Zhu Changluo was officially made heir-apparent, although his mother received no promotion in title until five years later, when her grandson Zhu Youjiao was born. By then, however, Wang had suffered for two decades in her cold palace. Constantly ill and nearly blind, Wang had lost faith in life itself. Her health grievously worsened in the 40th year of the Wanli reign (1612). Learning about this, the heir-apparent asked to visit his mother, but she refused her son's request. He had to break into her palace in order to see her. "Now that you've become heir-apparent," she said tearfully fingering a corner of his robe, "what other hopes can I cherish? Now I can die with no regrets." And she passed away shortly thereafter.

A funeral ceremony befitting Wang's new status was not held until the fifth day after her death, but it took place only after a specific proposal was made by court minister Ye Xianggao (1559-1627). Regarding the actual funeral ceremony, the Board of Rites proposed specific arrangements according to current imperial regulations, but no approval was forthcoming from the throne until the sixth day after the receipt of the Board's report, and this only came about thanks to the insistence of members of the imperial cabinet. Wang was buried at the foot of Mt. Tianshou (Heavenly

Longevity) but no officials were appointed to take care of her tomb; it was as if its occupant were a mere commoner. Wang was posthumously honoured as Empress Dowager during the reign of her grandson Zhu Youjiao, who ruled the Ming Dynasty as Emperor Tianqi (1621-1627). At that time her remains were moved to the Dingling, and a memorial hall built in her honour. Thus at long last an injustice was redressed for the beautiful and kind Lady Wang — but too late.

HIS IMPERIAL MAJESTY FALLS OVERBOARD

Wan Yi

When Zhu Youjiao of the Ming Dynasty mounted the throne as Emperor Tianqi (reigned 1621-1627), he was only 16 years old. The young emperor bestowed special favours on two persons: his wet nurse, Qie, and the eunuch Wei Zhongxian. Soon after his enthronement, he conferred on Qie the title of Lady of Great Service to His Imperial Majesty, and gave her the added honour of allowing her to reside in the Palace of Universal Tranquillity, the living quarters of queen mothers and empress dowagers, and of riding in sedan chairs on the palace grounds. Even her son, Hou Guoxing, was given an official post. The notorious toady Wei Zhongxian gained the emperor's trust during the latter's childhood, when Wei was an attendant in the imperial nursery.

After Emperor Tianqi assumed the throne, Qie and Wei began to work together to usurp power at court. Many upright ministers, eunuchs and imperial concubines lost their lives because of their machinations, and the common people, too, suffered from their tyranny. In fact, their wickedness and audacity were fuelled by Emperor Tianqi's stupidity. In the sixth month of the fourth year of Tianqi's reign, associate imperial censor Yang Lian and some of his colleagues jointly sent memorials to the emperor on the subject of Wei Zhongxian's crimes. The throne, however, had them arrested and thrown into prison where they died one after the next.

Being a dandy from childhood, the weak-willed emperor enjoyed practising horsemanship and watching operas featuring acrobatics. Rather than pay proper attention to state affairs, he spent most of his time on carpentry and building houses with his trusted eunuchs and officials. The completion of a house made him very happy, but he would soon have it demolished for amusement. He was often seen working stripped of his imperial robe. When absorbed in such labours, he "lost interest in drinking and eating and became oblivious to whether it was hot or cold out." Wei Zhongxian took advantage of such moments of inattention and report affairs of state to His Majesty. Reluctant to lay down his tools, the emperor would listen absent-mindedly and say, "All right, go ahead with your plan."

The emperor also took pleasure in playing with water. He would fill a large vat with water and put it on a tall stand. The water rushed through a hole drilled in the bottom of the vat and flowed into a second container designed to direct the jet like a fountain. Wooden balls the size of a walnut placed in the second container would spin, rise and fall in the gushing water, much to the delight of His Majesty. Wei and

Lady Qie seldom missed the opportunity to be on hand and acclaim the emperor's ingenuity.

One afternoon of the 18th day of the fifth month during the fifth year of his reign, Emperor Tianqi was amusing himself in the West Garden, present-day Beihai (Northern Sea) Park and Zhongnanhai Lake (Middle and Southern Sea). Although the empress had left His Majesty at about four o'clock, the latter continued rowing in a small pleasure boat near present-day Jade Flowery Isle in Beihai Park, accompanied by two young eunuchs. Meanwhile, Lady Qie and Wei Zhongxian were enjoying themselves nearby on a larger boat, drinking and chatting. Suddenly a strong gust of wind swept across the water, toppling His Majesty and the two eunuchs overboard together with a set of gold wine cups and pitchers. All those looking on, and Wei included, were at a loss what to do. Tan Jing, an older eunuch, jumped into the water and rescued the drenched and bedraggled "Son of Heaven". By the time Wei Zhongxian came to the emperor's aid, the emperor had been saved, but the two young eunuchs were drowned.

According to the etiquette of the time, Wei and Qie should have been punished severely for "negligence of duty". Yet Emperor Tianqi did nothing about it, and several months after the incident, he granted the pair gold seals and, a year later, conferred on the notorious eunuch the title of Venerable Duke. Even Wei's nephew, Liangqing, was promoted to the rank of a duke and given some 7,000 hectares of fertile land. The emperor went so far as to approve the building, in the imperial capital as well as other places, of temples in Wei's name, a rare honour for a living person.

With such a muddle-headed sovereign, the empire

naturally slid towards its demise. It was true that the succeeding emperor, Chongzhen (reigned 1628-1644), made short work of Lady Qie and the evil eunuch Wei, but by then it was too late. The Ming Dynasty fell in 1644.

THE TYRANNICAL EUNUCH WEI ZHONGXIAN

Fu Tongqin

The notorious Ming Dynasty eunuch Wei Zhongxian was a native of Suning in Hebei Province. In his youth, he never went to school and developed a reputation as a licentious scoundrel. He married, however, and had a daughter. Once when he lost in a gambling game, he was sneered at by his friends, and acting on impulse castrated himself. Soon after, he went to Beijing to seek his fortune, and found his way into the imperial court as a eunuch. Through bribery, he became a mess official serving the mother of the reigning Emperor Tianqi (reigned 1621-1627). He became the sworn brother of a eunuch named Wei Chao, a follower of the powerful senior eunuch Wang An, who had gained the trust of His Majesty. The two Weis competed in winning the hand of a woman named Qie, Emperor Tianqi's wet nurse. With the support of His Majesty, who knew very well that his former nurse loved Wei Zhongxian, the Hebei drunkard became Qie's "best friend", in spite of the fact that he was not properly equipped for the consummation of such a relationship. It was with her help that Wei Zhongxian rose to secretaryship in the Office of Court Ceremonials.

The Office of Court Ceremonials controlled the imperial seals, handled memorials to the throne from the court officials and made records of the sovereign's oral instructions before they became written imperial edicts. Scholarship was the chief qualification for employment there, yet the virtually illiterate Wei Zhongxian was recruited through his bizarre relations with Lady Qie.

Emperor Tianqi was not at all fond of study and spent much of his time tinkering with clever gadgets, building houses, doing carpentry, painting furniture and the like. Wei Zhongxian actively encouraged him "to develop his cultivation of music and dancing, and to play with animals and go hunting". Taking advantage of His Majesty's negligence of state affairs, he hatched numerous plots to usurp power, and became more and more overweening to the point of flouting the throne and court etiquette.

In the third year of the Tianqi reign, Wei Zhongxian organized 3,000 court eunuchs for military training with headquarters in the Five-Phoenix Tower on the grounds of the inner palace. He gave them regular training in horsemanship and use of weapons, and at one point staged a military parade witnessed by over 10,000 of his relatives and followers. The imperial palace was turned into a scene of great commotion, with the booming of drums and crashing of gongs. Some censors ventured to memorialize the emperor to order a stop to Wei's impertinency, but the throne lent them a deaf ear.

The proud eunuch enjoyed dressing up in martial

attire and riding a horse around the Forbidden City. One day he rode past a side hall where the emperor was being entertained by some of his concubines. Wei had the audacity to ignore the "Son of Heaven" by remaining on horseback. But His Majesty was angered by this insolence and shot Wei's stud to death with an arrow before returning to the inner palace fuming. The eunuch defended himself with the argument that he should be allowed to ride a horse on the palace grounds since he was allowed to train his eunuch army there. It was with the patient counsel of the other eunuchs that Wei apologized — reluctantly, of course — to the throne, replying hypocritically that "Your servant's ignorance of His Imperial Majesty's presence in the side hall that day deserved a punishment of death by 10,000 cuts".

Wei Zhongxian held all the members of the imperial cabinet in contempt. When a veteran minister, Ye Xianggao (1559-1627), recommended that Wei's enemy Wang Wenyan become a seventh-grade official, the eunuch fabricated a criminal charge against him and had Wang arrested and his residence searched. When academician Ding Qianxue of the Imperial College was critical of Wei's wrong-doings, the eunuch retaliated by having twenty of his henchmen "break into Ding's residence and arrest him, on an imperial decree". The scholar was "badly beaten by clubs and stones" and died not long afterwards. When Wan Jing, a senior secretary in the Department of Land Reclamation, impeached Wei Zhongxian for "usurping power and pursuing personal gains", the despotic eunuch ordered a group of his servants "to drag Wan out of his residence and insult him in public". The next day, Wan was hauled to the Meridian Gate of the imperial palace where he was furnished with one hundred strokes of the bamboo, from which he eventually died.

Backed by Lady Qie, Wei Zhongxian formed a coterie of more than 30 other eunuchs, while outside the palace he organized a clique of more than 80 sworn followers. Known as the "Eunuch Party", Wei's organization was comprised of the "Five Tigers", "Five Tiger Cubs", "Ten Dogs", "Ten Youngsters" and "40 Grandchildren". Through them, Wei's tentacles extended to nearly the whole cabinet and to several provinces, where a number of governors and viceroys became his underlings.

Heading the "Five Tiger Cubs", Wei's adopted son Cui Chengxiu (?-1627) had a hand in most of the tyrannical eunuch's conspiracies. He compiled lists of dissenters and of "potential followers" which he presented to his adoptive father. In this way he gained more of the old man's trust as a result of which Wei helped him get appointed as the Minister of War, the tutor to the heir-apparent and a post as imperial censor. Perhaps no one in Chinese history ever held so many major posts concurrently in the court.

Among Wei's "Five Tiger Cubs" were Xu Xianchun and Tian Ergeng, leaders of the secret-service organization known as the Brocade Uniform Imperial Guards. They had agents across the country, who kept an eye on anyone who raised the slightest criticism of Wei Zhongxian. Offenders and even suspects "were punished by being skinned or having their tongues cut out", and large numbers of them were murdered. The mere mention of the Brocade Uniform Imperial Guards sent a shiver of terror into people's hearts.

Zhou Yingqiu, an imperial censor and head of the "Ten Dogs", struck up an acquaintance with Wei Zhongxian's nephew, Wei Liangqing. The young Wei enjoyed the pig's feet which Zhou prepared with great skill, and in due course, Zhou earned himself the nickname the "Pig-feet Censor".

Li Lusheng, one of the "Ten Children", had friends among the high officials of the Boards of Civil Office and War. His influence in these important government departments grew so quickly that anyone seeking a position there needed to insinuate himself into Li's good graces.

Many court officials sought to be adopted by Wei Zhongxian, among them the noted scholar Ruan Dacheng, who later became a minister. Gu Bingqian, a senior cabinet councillor, also tried to obtain this honour for himself, but he was too old. His only choice now was to have his four sons acknowledge Wei as their "Venerable Grandfather", and this forced relationship proved to be a great boon to him. With the aid of Ruan Dacheng, a scholar named Wei Guangwei became Wei Zhongxian's "younger brother", and before long he was enlisted into the cabinet. To express his gratitude to his "elder brother", Wei Guangwei made a point of reporting to the powerful eunuch all the important activities in the cabinet.

Though illiterate, Wei Zhongxian had a powerful memory. He knew all the important contents of the major documents read out to him by his confidant Li Chaoqin. When the emperor had memorials from his ministers read to him in the Palace of Heavenly Purity, he chose Li Yongzhen, another of Wei's agents, to select the essential points. Li deliberately omitted those sections in which Wei was criticized. When His Majesty was too lazy to deal with such memorials, Wei Zhongxian gladly stepped in and took over.

Wei's birthday celebrations were big events in the palace. Though he was born on the 30th day of the first month, "warm-up" celebration activities began some two weeks earlier. "The Cinnabar Staircase of the Palace of Heavenly Purity was crowded with people who had come to bring gifts to Wei Zhongxian, take part in Buddhist rites or sign their names to the longevity scroll." On the 30th, the palace had to accommodate so many well-wishers that "the belts of the officials' robes rubbed against one another and their official seals could be heard clicking against one another. It was said that the crowding resulted in physical injuries." Wei Zhongxian was officially addressed as "Nine Thousand Years", but some flatterers called him "Nine Thousand Nine Hundred Years" (the emperor himself was addressed as "Ten Thousand Years").

In the sixth year of Tianqi's reign, Zhejiang governor Pan Ruzhen proposed to the throne that a temple be erected in honour of the "meritorious" Wei Zhongxian. His Majesty accepted this proposal and, moreover, named the future structure "Temple of Universal Benevolence". Constructing temples in Wei's honour soon became the fashion across the country, even though the eunuch was still alive, and it was regarded as a criterion of official loyalty to "Nine Thousand Years". The area for many kilometres around Beijing was studded with many such temples. The one built by Liu Zhao, prefect of Jizhou, was the most extravagant of all. Wei's statue was gilded with gold and his hat decorated with pendants of pearls, much like the image of an emperor. During the enshrinement ceremony, huge crowds of people paraded around the spot, kowtowing in unison every few paces and shouting "Nine Thousand Years!" Some officials even made statues from precious *gharu* wood. "The entrails of the sculpture were made of gold, jade and other precious stones, and it was dressed in a splendid and gorgeous costume. An opening was left in the coiled hair where fresh flowers could be inserted."

The construction of these temples cost as much as hundreds of thousands taels of silver, and to make way for their construction numerous trees were felled and large numbers of civilian houses demolished. According to historical records, the building of a particular temple in Kaifeng required that more than 2,000 houses be pulled down, while one in Linqing (in Shandong Province) called for the destruction of more than 10,000 houses. In some places, the temples contained nine-bay palatial buildings faced with glazed titles like those in the Forbidden City. In rituals carried out in his honour, Wei was ranked on a par with the emperor.

These practices were opposed by a number of honest officials including Hu Shirong of the Jizhou Intendancy and Geng Ruqi of the Zunhua Intendancy, both of whom died at Wei's hands.

In the fourth year of the Tianqi reign, associate censor Yang Lian wrote the emperor a memorial listing twenty-four crimes which Wei Zhongxian had committed, some of them in collaboration with Lady Qie. These included persecuting imperial concubines and other eunuchs, training eunuchs on the palace grounds, violating ancestral rites, usurping power, eliminating dissidents, promoting personal followers, cheating and killing common people, and building temples in his honour throughout the country. "There is no matter, large or small, in the palace or in the government, that is not decided solely by Wei Zhongxian," Yang Lian pointed out. "Your Majesty have become a mere figurehead, for the real power of the government is in Wei's hands." When Wei's man Wang Tiqian read this memorial to the emperor, he took care to eliminate the most important parts, and Wei and Lady Qie managed to explain away the rest. A few days later, the following remarks were written in the emperor's vermilion ink on Yang's memorial: "The sovereign decides everything in affairs of the empire. How has the memorialist come to know so much about the Inner Palace?" Some time afterwards, Wei Dazhong, a supervisory official in the Board of Civil Office, and a dozen of his colleagues sent a joint memorial to the throne impeaching Wei Zhongxian and suggesting capital punishment for Wei and Lady Qie. Eventually, both Yang Lian and Wei Dazhong met with reprisals.

Wei Zhongxian had his men compile a list of all the court officials, dividing them into two categories. Those not belonging to the "Eunuch Party" were indicated by black dots over their names, while those supporting Wei's clique were marked with small circles. The list was duplicated so that each of Wei's followers could keep a copy in their sleeves when going to the imperial court. Using this list as a guide, they could keep tabs on the political leanings of all memorialists, and thus decide upon their promotion or demotion. Small wonder that Wei succeeded in reducing nearly the entire civil service to abject servility.

One way Wei Zhongxian dispatched his enemies

was to accuse them of belonging to the Donglin Party, which advocated reform and launched a moral crusade against the sycophants and time-servers who held the reins of power. When veteran minister Ye Xianggao recommended Wang Wenyan for a middle-ranking post, Wang was imprisoned on the trumped-up charge that he was a Donglin partisan. Several means of torture were tried on Wang: squeezing his fingers between sticks, flogging, sandwiching his head between wooden boards, crushing his limbs on a wooden bench and the like. When Wang resisted these various tortures, Wei's secret-service man Xu Xianchun fabricated a confession on his behalf and had him executed. The "Eunuch Party" perpetrated the Incident of the Six Gentlemen, among whom Yang Lian and Wei Dazhong, who were arrested on false charges. While in prison, "they were subjected to personal insult by being forced to take off their clothes, and tortu'ed by having their fingers squeezed between sticks and their bodies wedged between wooden boards. Sometimes they were forced to wear handcuffs and fetters while they were being tortured. Their bodily injuries had hardly healed before they were subjected to fresh torture. They all suffered so greatly that they were unable to kneel when interrogated, and had to lie on the floor." None of the six gentlemen survived the ordeal. Even when Yang Lian was breathing his last, his torturers pressed heavy sacks of earth on his abdomen and drove iron nails through his ears. In a matter of three years, scores of loyal officials were either tortured to death in prison or banished to the border regions, while over 300 others were dismissed from office and many more forced to resign.

In the seventh year of Emperor Tianqi's rule, Wei Zhongxian deceived the throne and heaped more honours on himself by submitting a fictitious report of military achievements in Liaodong. He arranged for one of his younger brothers to become the hereditary director of the palace secret-service organization, the Brocade Uniform Imperial Guards. By then, Wei himself had become head of the biggest terror network in the empire, the Eastern Depot. Some of his nephews were promoted in rank: Liangqing was made grand tutor to the heir-apparent; Mingwang, junior tutor to the heir-apparent; and the three-year-old Liangdong, Marquis of Dong'an. Even his two-year-old grandnephew, Pengyi, was granted the hereditary title of Earl of Ping'an. Lady Qie, to whom Wei was so intimately attached, benefited from the eunuch's meteoric rise by receiving quantities of gold coins and additional honours from the throne. Wei Zhongxian was in virtual control of the whole court — and much beyond it.

Early in the eighth month of the same year, Emperor Tianqi fell seriously ill. Wei took advantage of his infirmity to fabricate imperial edicts and promote his relatives and supporters to higher and more lucrative posts. On the 22nd, Tianqi died, and he was succeeded on the throne by his brother, who reigned as Emperor Chongzhen (1628-1644).

Soon after his enthronement, Chongzhen received a joint memorial from Lu Chengyuan and Qian Yuanque, under-secretaries of the Boards of Works and Civil Office respectively, impeaching Wei Zhongxian. In response, the notorious eunuch requested to be relieved of his leadership of the Eastern Depot, which the new emperor disapproved, though he found it appropriate to banish Lady Qie from the inner palace. Then Qian Jia-zheng, a senior licentiate from Zhejiang, brought a charge against Wei, listing ten crimes: "One, usurping the power of the throne; two, insulting the empress; three, seizing military power; four defying ancestral practices; five, weakening border defences; six, desecrating the memory of ancient sages; seven, abusing official titles; eight, arrogating to himself others' meritorious service in border defence; nine, exploiting the common people; and ten, offering bribes." Emperor Chongzhen dismissed Wei from his palace positions and sent him to Fengyang to look after the Ming emperors' ancestors' tombs. Flaunting his remaining power, however, the evil eunuch set out for Fengyang with his personal possessions borne by a thousand stallions and guarded by nearly 800 soldiers. This aroused the indignation of the court ministers who petitioned the emperor on the subject of Wei's effrontery as follows: "Wei Zhongxian deserves death for usurping state power and persecuting loyal officials. His being sent to Fengyang is indeed light punishment. Yet he refuses to admit his evil deeds and has allowed his desperate followers accompany him to Fengyang, in their way displaying his authority and defying the throne." Before long, the new emperor ordered Wei to return to the capital. Fearing the worst fate for his monstrous crimes, he committed suicide en route. "An imperial decree ordered that Wei Zhongxian's corpse be dismembered and his head displayed on the city gate of Hejian County, Hebei Province near where he killed himself." His family property was confiscated and then sold, the proceeds being used for military expenses. At the same time, Lady Qie's family property met the same fate, and the cruel woman was beaten to death.

For their own crimes, Wei Zhongxian and Lady Qie's henchmen received their due punishments in the form of execution, exile, or forced labour. Others were demoted or removed from office. The relatives of the sinister pair were also penalized according to circumstances. Imperial concubines who had been victimized by the scheming eunuch and Lady Qie were rehabilitated as were officials who died at their hands. Those opponents of theirs who survived the reign of terror were recalled to power.

"Events reverse themselves when they reach extremes" — this was what the court official Wu Huaixian wrote in an essay commemorating the death of the Six Gentlemen who had been persecuted to death by Wei Zhongxian. Wu himself met the same fate not long after that, but his prediction became a reality when the cold-blooded eunuch hanged himself after seven years of dictatorial rule.

EMPEROR KANGXI ARRESTS A VICIOUS COUNCILLOR BY STRATEGY

Li Zhiting

Chinese history records countless incidents of struggle in the imperial courts, some of them bloody and others battles of wits. A classic example of the latter is the rivalry between Emperor Kangxi (reigned 1662-1722) and his influential councillor Aobai, as a result of which the throne wrested back its imperial power.

Aisin Gioro Xuanye was a mere child of six when he was placed on the throne to succeed his father, Emperor Shunzhi (reigned 1644-1661), as Emperor Kangxi. To assist the boy sovereign in the administration of the vast empire, Emperor Shunzhi wrote a will on his deathbed, naming four of his most trusted high ministers Suoni, Sukesaha, Ebilong and Aobai (all were Manchu nobles) as Imperial Regent Councillors. According to the *Draft History of the Qing Dynasty*, they accepted the task by taking the following oath, which was read outloud by Suoni, the oldest of the four: "Suoni and his three colleagues hereby pledge their loyalty to the throne and their readiness to give up their lives to assist His Majesty in governing the empire. They vow that they will never confer special benefits upon their relatives or friends, harbour personal grievances against anyone, seek ill-gotten wealth, be influenced by any of those near and dear to them, take bribes, or form cliques for selfish purposes. They will act in the capacity of loyal Imperial Regent Councillors to repay the trust placed in them by the deceased sovereign."

Before very long, however, Aobai seemed to have forgotten everything in the collective oath. He became extremely arrogant, putting on airs of a veteran who had rendered great service to the dynasty. Most of the court officials, both civilian and military, dreaded him. Soon after his appointment to his new post, he used his power to persecute those who refused to obey him. In one case, Feiyanggu, a meritorious imperial bodyguard, died as the result of a scheme of Aobai's making.

Aobai had wild ambitions and tried to arrogate all power vested in the four councillors to himself, though his position was the lowest among them. Suoni, who among the four had the highest rank and had served the empire the longest, was too old and physically weak to do much about Aobai. Ebilong was prudent, never venturing to differ from Aobai in any matter. The recalcitrant Sukesaha was the only councillor who dared argue with his despotic colleague. Before long he became a thorn in Aobai's flesh, and felt the growing pressure Aobai brought to bear on him.

In the sixth year of his reign, 14-year-old Kangxi took the reins of government in his own hands. Sukesaha petitioned to be allowed to retire so that he could pay more visits to the mausoleum of the late Emperor Shunzhi. The reason behind this gesture was that he found it increasingly difficult to work with Aobai and, moreover, he wanted to hint to Aobai that he should be wise enough to mend his ways. Correctly intuiting the meaning behind Sukesaha's request, Aobai was furious and began to plot against him. He fabricated 24 criminal charges against Sukesaha and his eldest son Chakedan, an imperial bodyguard, and sentenced them to dismemberment; while Sukesaha's six other sons, one grandson, two nephews and two relatives (Bai'erhetu, a general; and Erde, an imperial guard) were sentenced to beheading. Having gotten wind of the conflict between Aobai and Sukesaha, Emperor Kangxi rescinded Aobai's memorial ordering the executions. The tyrannical councillor came and argued face to face with His Majesty, who at first refused to change his mind. Thoroughly enraged, Aobai shouted and waved his fist at the young emperor, who finally bowed to the old rascal's demands, with the one modification — in consideration of the accused's contributions to the Qing house — that Sukesaha be hanged instead of dismembered.

Having despatched his arch enemy, Aobai became more overbearing and unscrupulous. On New Year's Day of the eighth year of Kangxi's reign (1669), all the ministers assembled at court to extend their greetings to the throne. Aobai, who stood at the head of this assembly, was wearing a yellow robe exactly like His Majesty's, the only difference being that Aobai had a ball of red wool on his official cap while the emperor's crown was decorated with a giant pearl. Aobai's effrontery was on a scale seldom seen in the entire history of the imperial court.

With Aobai's tentacles stretched in all directions,

Emperor Kangxi was relegated to the status of a figure-head. Aobai had an extensive coterie under his control, and his followers and relatives were planted throughout all departments of the government. In fact, he dominated all six metropolitan boards. All major issues from the appointment of high-ranking officials to the enforcement of imperial policies were discussed and decided upon in Aobai's residence and only afterwards reported to the throne. Kangxi had little choice but to swallow these insults — at least for the time being.

When it became clear that the Aobai clique presented a serious threat to Kangxi's authority, the sovereign resolved to blot it out. Cautious, well-planned action was necessary in view of the fact that Aobai effectively monopolized both the military and civil power structures, and had installed his own henchmen at all levels of government.

The emperor sought the advice of his loyal guard Suo'etu, Suoni's son. Then, under the pretext of having a number of people keep him company during recreational hours, His Majesty recruited a dozen robust and clever Manchu youngsters. They were taught wrestling and martial arts, sometimes directly under Aobai's nose. At times His Majesty would even join them in their exercises. Seeing all this, the scoundrel inwardly congratulated himself. "After all," he thought, "Kangxi is a child who only knows how to play." The emperor's apparent lack of political ambition was precisely what Aobai anticipated in his scheme to usurp additional power. To further lower Aobai's guard, Kangxi began to show more respect to him.

Before long the dozen youngsters became Kangxi's most trusted attendants. One day in the fifth month of the eighth year of his reign (1669), Kangxi ordered a private audience with Aobai. Aobai arrived at the imperial palace, swaggering as usual. Just as he was stepping over the threshold, a number of youngsters jumped out from the sides of the gateway and fell on him. He was pinned to the ground and arrested before he knew what had happened.

Aobai was handed over to Prince Kang for trial. Meanwhile, his followers were arrested one after another. Aobai was found guilty of thirty criminal counts, all of which he confessed to before the emperor. The court was unanimous in demanding that Aobai be sentenced to death. In recognition of his previous useful service to the empire, however, the throne was lenient to him, reducing his sentence to life imprisonment. Aobai's chief followers were all beheaded. Soon afterwards, Kangxi issued an imperial decree rehabilitating all the court ministers who had been hounded to death by Aobai.

Kangxi's astute move gave a face-lift to the early Qing regime.

EMPEROR QIANLONG BUILDS A GOLD STUPA TO PRESERVE HIS MOTHER'S HAIR

Liu Guilin

Preserving the hair of great historical figures or of one's ancestors has long been regarded in China as a sign of respect. It is said that ten stupas were erected in India to preserve the relics of Gautama Buddha, one of them exclusively for his hair. In China, Emperor Qianlong (reigned 1736-1795) of the Qing Dynasty spent more than 3,000 taels of gold to have an exquisite stupa made to store his mother's fallen hair.

Qianlong's mother died in the first month of the forty-second year of his reign (1777) at the age of 86. Within less than one month of her death, the emperor issued an order saying, "To show our respect for the hair of Her Majesty the Empress Dowager, I hereby order that a gold stupa be built, with an image of the Buddha Amitabha enshrined within." At the same time, only a little more than 1,300 taels of gold were available for the purpose, in the form of one gold scroll, one gold seal, a number of gold ingots in the Garden of Pleasant Spring, and the gold cooking utensils lying unused in the Palace of Vigorous Old Age. Given the amount of gold available, the Department of Imperial Court Affairs made a model of the stupa out of *nanmu* (*phoebe nanmu*) 2.16 *chi*** in height. Since the statue of Amitabha was too large to fit inside it, however, Emperor Qianlong, who prided himself on his filial piety, ordered that a larger model be made. He did not specify the exact height, nor did he bother about the actual amount of gold needed.

Prior to this, a number of gold memorial pagodas had been constructed in the Forbidden City, such as the two small pagodas in the Western Meditation Hall of the Palace of Double Glory and a larger one in the Pavilion of Fragrant Clouds near the Hall of Uprightness. Recalling these things when discussing the size of the Amitabha statue, Qianlong ordered General Jin Hui to check on the quantity of gold used to cast the three above-mentioned pagodas. The next day, he gave a similar order to Longfu'an, head of the Imperial Court Affairs Department. A joint report was submitted to His Majesty a couple of days later, in which it was stated that the two pagodas in the Palace of Double Glory had heights of 4.6 *chi* and required a combined total of 4,960.7 taels of gold, while the one in the Hall of Uprightness was 16 *chi* in height and required 11,119.9 taels of gold. When Jin Hui and Longfu'an proposed that the gold pots, spoons, chopsticks and other utensils stored in the Palace of Vigorous Old Age and the gold ingots in the warehouse of the Imperial Court Affairs Department be turned over to the Construction Depart-

---

* *Chi* is a unit of length equal to approximately 1.1 feet.

ment for casting the stupa, Qianlong immediately gave his approval. This brought the total amount of gold to 2,300 taels, which was still not enough for the planned stupa. To make up the difference, Longfu'an requisitioned 700.63 taels of silver, when smelted together with the gold would produce 3,009.98 taels of an alloy with a gold content of sixty per cent. This was sufficient to construct a gold stupa of the required size.

The pagoda was finally completed on the third day of the 11th month of the same year. During the nine-month period that intervened, His Majesty went to the trouble of issuing twenty orders related to the pagoda. It took him more than a month to consider and finalize the details of the model structure. He sent down nine rescripts on the subject of collecting gold and silver, making the model and appointing officials to supervise the actual construction. It was recorded that three orders came from the throne on the third day of the third month alone: one for enlarging the model; another inquiring about the purity of the gold to be used; yet another investigating the amount of gold used in the three existing pagodas.

Once the wooden model for the gold stupa was approved by the emperor on the second day of the fourth month, the work of casting began under the supervision of Foning and Si'de, senior secretary and councillor respectively, of the Imperial Court Affairs Department. To discourage any dishonest practices or waste in the handling of the gold or any loafing on the part of the craftsmen, Taining and Pingde, senior secretaries of the Boards of Works and Revenue respectively, were ordered to oversee the project. Particular attention was paid to the prescribed thickness of the gold applied. Emperor

Qianlong demanded progress reports on every single detail of the stupa's construction from its base to the umbrella-like structure at its peak. The manufacture of the gold casket which was to contain the Empress Dowager's hair went through the same complex procedure of imperial approval as the stupa itself. Even the designs of the sandalwood pedestals for the casket and the Mt. Sumeru platform for the stupa itself had to be passed by His Majesty before construction could begin.

After more than three months of hectic work, a five-storeyed gold stupa 4.6 *chi* in height and with a base of 2.2 square *chi* was completed ahead of schedule. There is no way to calculate how much painstaking labour went into this gracefully designed structure. More than two centuries old, it is now on display in the Exhibition Halls of Rare Treasures in the Palace Museum in Beijing.

PALACE MAID BEATEN TO DEATH BY AN IMPERIAL CONCUBINE

Zuo Buqing

The keeping of bondservants was a common practice during the Qing Dynasty, with the families of feudal nobles, bureaucrats or landlords owning scores of them. During the Qianlong reign (1736-1795), a county magistrate might even own hundreds of them, and Grand Secretary Heshen (1750-1799) boasted as many as 1,000 or more. They could be exploited, tortured, sold or even given away as gifts according to their masters' wishes. Large numbers of them died as a result of inhuman treatment. In a memorial to the throne, Zhu Zhibi, Minister of Punishments, wrote, "Every year, this board receives reports of no less than two thousand cases of bondservants in Bannermen's families committing suicide. Are these people dying for no reason? A lack of proper education and material comforts, or physical torment exacerbated by cold and hunger, forces them to end their lives nursing a grievance. This has become an inevitable trend."

Stripped of its formality, this statement means that bondservants were hounded to death by their masters. In the sixth year of the Qianlong period, Grand Secretary Fumin's grandson, Fuhai, beat his bondman Chang De to death, after which he dismembered and burnt his corpse. Even the emperor himself thought this "beyond heavenly principles and human sensibilities". It is true that the preceding sovereign Yongzheng (reigned 1723-1735) decreed that those officials who beat their bondservants to death for no good reason be subjected to three kinds of punishment, depending on the case: fines, demotion, and flogging. These penalties, however, remained merely paper threats throughout the Yongzheng reign.

As the epitome of the feudal ruling class, the imperial family owned the largest number of chattel attendants who provided the onerous labour that made the luxurious palace life possible, but who were punished or even put to death on the slightest pretext. In the 43rd year of Qianlong's reign, Imperial Concubine Dun beat one of her bondwomen so severely that she died shortly afterwards. The emperor dealt with this case personally, for, in his own words, it involved "excess and indiscriminate torture and improper treatment of palace maids". The day after the incident, the emperor summoned the princes and grand councillors to the Western Warm Chamber of the Hall of Mental Cultivation. "Imperial Concubine Dun," he declared, "will be demoted by one grade as a warning to others." He admonished his other concubines to learn a lesson from this and to avoid similar punishment. "Although certain maids of honour committed suicide in the past because my concubines were bad-tempered and beat them too harshly, something I do not approve of," he said. "No maid has ever died of severe beating. With the case of Imperial Concubine Dun before me, I cannot but deal with it sternly; otherwise it would be contrary to common justice, and the case itself would fail to serve as a warning to my other consorts. Since all court officials, be they of Han or Manchu nationality, who fail to punish their family servants according to law and beat them to death, will be penalized by dismissal from office or demotion accordingly, how can I afford to shield those consorts of mine who violate the existing regulations?"

Dun had been promoted to the rank of imperial concubine in the 32nd year of the Qianlong reign (1767). She bore the emperor a daughter who later became the daughter-in-law of Grand Secretary Heshen. Dun should have been severely punished for ill-treatment of her maid, but according to Emperor Qianlong himself, "Leniency might be shown to her because she has brought up a princess. Considering the specific circumstances, downgrading her rank cannot be considered too severe." Qianlong had the cheek to cite himself as a good example: "Though I am master of all under heaven and hold power over their lives, I have never once arbitrarily caned any of my eunuchs to death." When junior eunuchs Hu Shijie and Ruyi offended him, he added, "I only punished them lightly, giving them 20 or at most 40 strokes of the bamboo." He cautioned the princes "to do as I do in handling family affairs involving your consorts and daughters, rather than practising favouritism. A princess, as well as your consorts and daughters, should guard against giving in to your temper and indiscriminately punishing servants."

All others involved in the death of Imperial Concubine Dun's maid were punished. Guo Jinzhong and Liu Liang, the eunuchs in charge of Dun's palace, were deprived of their official cap decorations indicating their respective ranks and fined two years' grain levies; while Wang Zhong, Wang Cheng, Zheng Yuzhu and Zhao Desheng, all eunuchs in charge of the Inner Palace, were fined one year's grain levies for failure to dissuade Dun from committing the offence. Since they were not directly responsible for Dun's wrongdoing, however, Emperor Qianlong ordered that half of these fines be borned by Dun herself. The imperial concubine was also ordered to pay one hundred taels of silver to cover burial expenses for the dead maid. The emperor had his decision on the case transmitted to the minister in charge of the Imperial Court Affairs Department, and ordered that copies be made and distributed to the offices of the cabinet and the chief eunuch.

In directly intervening for the case of the death of an ordinary palace maid, Qianlong was attempting to demonstrate his impartiality and prove that "he had all along refrained from doing anything out of personal consideration during the past 43 years of his reign". He added, "When my ministers perform well, I will reward them. When they do wrong, I will reprimand them. . . . Can a sovereign rule his empire if he is unable to act in this way?"

It turned out, however, that Qianlong's statement was little more than self-glorification. For Imperial Concubine Dun was restored her former rank not long after the case was closed.

AN UNFORTUNATE ASSASSIN

Zhang Shucai

In 1803, an unemployed cook tried to assassinate the Qing Emperor Jiaqing, although neither official nor unofficial histories of the Qing court give a detailed, authentic account of this much discussed case. A number of unique documents now preserved in Beijing's No. 1 Historical Archives enable us to solve a mystery which has baffled historians until modern times.

MISERABLE LIFE

The would-be assassin, named Chen De, was born in Beijing in 1757, the twenty-second year of the Qianlong reign. He spent his childhood in Shandong Province, where his parents were pawned as servants in a number of officials' homes. When he was old enough, Chen too worked as a servant for wealthy families, besides doing odd jobs as well.

Chen returned to Beijing at the age of 31, shortly after his parents' death. Then, foᴌ some eight years he and his wife worked in turn as domestics for an imperial guard, a secretary in the Board of Punishments and a clerk in the Department of Imperial Court Affairs. In 1796, 39-year-old Chen De became an orderly in the latter department, and was entrusted with making sundry purchases for the imperial palace and helping with the transport of household items when the emperor and his empress and concubines visited the Yuanmingyuan (Old Summer Palace) in the capital's western suburbs. It was at this time that Chen became familiar with the layout of the Forbidden City. In the third year of the subsequent Jiaqing period, he and his wife were employed as cooks by a retired official in Beijing. Five years later, his wife and sister died in turn, and his mother-in-law, whom he supported, became crippled. Poverty drove him to the brink of madness, and he took to drinking, often wailing and laughing uncontrollably when he had exceeded his normal capacity. As a result, Chen was fired by his new master within one year. His unsuccessful assassination of Emperor Jiaqing took place on the 20th day of the second intercalary month of that leap year (1803), when Chen was 47.

Chen De's attempt on the sovereign's life had been simmering in his mind for some time. Four days before he struck, Chen noticed the main street leading to the rear gate of the Forbidden City being cleaned and paved with fresh earth. It was not difficult for him to learn the exact date of the emperor's return to the imperial palace after his brief visit to the Yuanmingyuan.

On the morning of the 20th day of that second intercalary month, Chen De started drinking heavily in a wine shop near the eastern wall of the palace. With him was his elder son Lu'er, who was 15. Father and son then proceeded to rear palace gate, the Gate of Divine Might, through which they slipped into the Forbidden City. After observing the deployment of the imperial guards, they concealed themselves behind a high wall in the western part of the palace.

Before long, Emperor Jiaqing entered the Gate of Divine Might, riding on a lavishly decorated sedan chair. As he was approaching the Gate of Obedience and Chastity, Chen De darted out from his hiding place and charged at him, dagger in hand. Caught totally unprepared by the sudden appearance of an assassin, the emperor jumped off his chair and ran towards the inner gate. None of the more than one hundred guards on both flanks were quick enough to block Chen's way, and only Mian'en, the Prince Ding, the emperor's son-in-law Lawangduo'erji, and four imperial bodyguards made any attempt to stop the assassin who, flailing his weapon wildly, wounded one of the bodyguards and slashed Prince Ding's sleeve before he was arrested.

In his confession, Chen De explained his motives as follows: "I was so frustrated by my poverty that I decided to try and turn my misfortune into fortune by making a surprise assault on His Majesty. . . . In the second year of the Jiaqing reign, I had a dream in which my friend Wang Fu ushered me into an imperial palace. The next year, I had another dream in which I was lying under a bridge on a dried up riverbed. When I was helped to my feet and stepped onto the bridge, I found myself clad in a dragon-patterned robe. Afterwards, I read a book which gave me the idea that I was possibly destined to be an emperor. . . . One day several years ago, I had my fortune told. I drew five bamboo slips from the 'divination box', and the inscriptions on them all augured well. . . . By and by, I lost my self-control and decided to try my luck. . . . Also, I believed I was sufficiently well trained in the martial arts."

It is apparent that Chen De tried to assassinate Emperor Jiaqing because — first, poverty had driven him mad; second, dreams and divination led him to start imagining things; and third, he fancied his skill in the martial arts could help him accomplish his purpose. But perhaps the principal cause of his action was abject poverty. As Chen admitted, "I felt more and more frustrated, as if I were going to explode."

TRIAL AND EXECUTION

After Chen De's arrest, Emperor Jiaqing immediately ordered the Grand Council and the Board of Punishments to interrogate and try him. Later, the Grand Secretaries and the ministers of the other five metropolitan boards joined the trial in the course of which Chen was cross-examined day and night for several days while being subjected to kneeling on chains, flogging, pressing between thick rods, etc. He remained undaunted throughout, repeating his vows to unthrone the emperor. Between tortures, he told the court he had tried to kill himself several times because life was too hard for him and his family. And he recounted before his torturers his bitter experiences in serving different masters. When asked why he chose to assassinate the emperor rather than commit suicide in a quiet corner, he said, "What purpose would killing myself that way serve? By wounding the imperial guards and then rushing up to His Majesty on his sedan chair, I showed people that even the 'Son of Heaven' was under my thumb."

Chen De's case attracted the attention of the whole court. Torture was applied repeatedly to force him to reveal his "instigators, accomplices and followers". His two sons, friends whose names he mentioned during the trial and all those whom he had served were pressed for further information. His sons and friends claimed to know nothing about his assassination plans, and all his former masters testified that he was a quiet servant who knew his place and who had no contact with any dubious people. After four days and four nights, Chen's inquisitors concluded that his act was "an isolated case of attempting to the imperial throne", and that he was "an unemployed servant whose wicked thoughts were derived from dreams and the ill effects of divination". A report was submitted to the throne and punishment proposed. In his comments on the report, Emperor Jiaqing wrote, "It is a poor idea to extract confessions by torture, because it easily causes criminals to act like a mad dog and implicate others, whereupon those so named will suffer. If there were no interrogation, however, the case would remain a mystery and enormous losses result. What is most disturbing is the worsening quality of social morality, and this assassination attempt on my life must have been due to a lack of adequate benevolence on my part. I should therefore review my conduct and strive to be more discreet, cultivate my character more conscientiously, attend to affairs of state more diligently and cherish the populace more sincerely than before." Later that intercalary month, Chen De was put to slow death by dismemberment, and his two sons hanged.

According to *The Draft History of the Qing Dynasty*, Chen faced death stoically. "Having been carted to the execution ground, Chen De was tied to a stake. His two sons were brought to him and made to kowtow in front of their father before being hanged. He closed his eyes. Then his own execution began. The executioner cut slices of flesh from his ears, nose, chest, left and right arms and back, applying the knife as if scaling a fish. Blood streamed down his body at first, but after the bleeding stopped, only a yellowish liquid oozed out. When all the flesh of the upper part of his body had been removed, Chen De opened his eyes and shouted, 'Cut more quickly!' The official supervising his execution told him, 'His Majesty has decreed that you suffer as long as possible.' Chen closed his eyes again and remained silent until his death."

While Chen De's attempt on the emperor's life as a way of escape from his miserable lot was doubtless impractical and doomed to failure, the incident itself, the first assassination attempt on a Qing sovereign inside the heavily guarded Forbidden City, produced a great impact on the feudal court.

Firstly, the case shocked the ruling class. Apart from ordering a joint trial by all the central boards and key departments and having him executed by the cruelest method, Emperor Jiaqing issued a special decree on the security of the throne: "All places where I live or stay are forbidden areas. Accordingly, the Yuanmingyuan, Rehe Mountain Resort and the Mulan Hunting Grounds are no different from the imperial palace itself. . . .

The throne should be strictly guarded, and when I am travelling my guards and attendants should stay as near to me as possible." Jiaqing instructed the Ministers of the Imperial Presence, the Grand Councillors, the commander of the Imperial Guards, his military commanders and the ministers in charge of the Department of Imperial Court Affairs to work out measures to safeguard the emperor as well as the entire palace.

Secondly, Chen De's attempt sowed seeds of mistrust and conflict among the ruling cliques. Emperor Jiaqing tried to seek out Chen's possible instigators and accomplices because he suspected someone among the imperial officials might have been pulling strings behind the scenes. For "negligence of duty", all 17 officials and officers stationed at the Gate of Divine Might and the Eastern Flowery Gate were sentenced to forced labour, dismissed from office, demoted, transferred or fined. Several leaders of the imperial guards were cashiered and paraded in the cangue before being handed over to their respective units for severe penalties. Even Prince Su, supervisor of palace security work, was sent to the Department of Imperial Household Affairs for punishment. Expressing his anger over the incident, Emperor Jiaqing said, "As the sovereign of the empire, I have been sincere to my ministers and trust them fully. I regard all my officials as members of my own household. How, then, could they have allowed an assassin to attack me? . . . Could it be that among the more than 100 onlookers, there is no one to whom I am near and dear? Are they not all my servants who have benefited from my imperial favour? If they show such indifference at such an incident, can they be expected to perform their official tasks with loyalty? This worries me more than the incident itself. If they still retain a shred of conscience and ask themselves, will they not feel ashamed of the way they behaved that day?"

Thirdly, having executed Chen De and his two sons and having punished all the officials and officers concerned, Emperor Jiaqing felt he had to make a gesture of self-examination and make his "deficiencies" "known to the empire and the world at large". All this was designed to mitigate the social contradictions that had been intensifying under his reign.

THE MURDER OF THE
RELIEF FUND INSPECTOR

Zhang Mingxin and Li Guilian

In 1809 the reigning Jiaqing Emperor wrote a long poem in praise of Li Yuchang, a successful candidate in the metropolitan civil-service examinations who had been murdered by a corrupt official while overseeing the distribution of relief funds. By imperial decree, a stone tablet inscribed with the text of this poem was erected in front of Li's tomb. The story of this peculiar murder has been compiled from the biographical section of *The Draft History of the Qing Dynasty, The Factual Records of the Qing Period* and other sources.

A SCHOLAR APPOINTED RELIEF
FUND INSPECTOR

The Huanghe (Yellow) River, China's sorrow, often overflowed its banks during the Qing Dynasty. The 13th year of the Jiaqing period (1808) witnessed a particularly disastrous inundation centring on Huai'an Prefecture in Jiangsu Province resulting in large numbers of peasants being rendered homeless and dying of famine. To alleviate social unrest and forestall popular insurrection, the imperial government was forced to set aside as relief funds some of the wealth it had taken from the common people. Corruption, however, was rife, so much so that officials handling relief funds and grain generously lined their pockets, "grabbing food from the mouths of the starving masses". Even the emperor himself regretted this situation: "It is hard for the imperial beneficence to reach every corner of the whole empire due to the officials' vicious ways." In these circumstances, the honest scholar-official Li Yuchang stood out like a crane among the chickens, as a Chinese idiom puts it.

A native of Jimi County, Shandong Province, Li passed the highest imperial examinations in the 13th year of the Jiaqing rule. He became an official the same year, and was charged with overseeing the distribution of relief funds for Shanyang Prefecture in Jiangsu Province.

The magistrate of Shanyang was Wang Shenhan, a man who was blinded by lust for gain and "broke the bones of the people and sucked their marrow". He regularly inflated the actual number of victims of natural calamities in order to request additional funds and materials, some of which he took for himself. In 1808 alone, he embezzled 25,000 taels of silver out of a total 90,000 taels earmarked for his county.

After arriving in Shanyang, Li Yuchang made the rounds of the local villages to familiarize himself with the extent of the flood damage. He was shocked by the grim realities he saw, with numerous victims struggling on the verge of starvation. Back in his office, he carefully checked the registers of the county's residents and found evidence of serious misreporting. Highly indignant, he drafted a report to the provincial treasurer.

Suffering a guilty conscience, Wang Shenhan ordered one of his *yamen* runners, Bao Xiang, to ingratiate himself with Li Xiang, one of Li Yuchang's servants. Li Xiang, who had been hoping to enrich himself by serving a relief fund inspector, was now disgruntled because his master proved to be an honest official who was exacting with subordinates. Reading Li's thoughts, Bao Xiang roped the servant in by lavish promises of material gain. Thus Wang Shenhan was able to learn that Li Yuchang was planning to expose his embezzlement of flood relief money.

AN ATTEMPTED MURDER

As it was the general rule at the time for bureaucrats to shield one another, Wang Shenhan assumed that Li Yuchang's plan was merely blackmail, and that everything would be all right if he offered Li part of the spoils. Wang then asked a friend of his to tell Li that he would be the recipient of 10,000 taels of silver if he were willing to cover up Wang's embezzlement. Wang never expected that Li would flatly refuse his offer and insist on handling the matter in the proper manner. Moreover, the Shandong scholar was ready to lay bare before the provincial treasurer the magistrate's scheme to bribe him and suggest additional penalties for his crime.

Unreconciled to his bad luck, Wang Shenhan discussed his next move with Bao Xiang. Bao suggested buying over Li Xiang and having him steal the register of famine victims from Li Yuchang and burning it. The magistrate agreed.

When Bao related the new plan to Li Xiang, the latter approved of it but he said that he needed the help of Gu Xiang and Ma Liansheng, two other servants in Li Yuchang's employ. Generous bribery secured their collaboration. Their only difficulty was that Li Yuchang took such good care of all official documents that the three unscrupulous servants failed in their repeated attempts to steal them.

Staking everything on a single throw, Wang Shenhan decided to get rid of Li Yuchang. He asked Bao Xiang to tell Li's servants that they would each be rewarded with a large sum of money plus an official position for their co-operation in this plan. Heady with prospects of gain, the three willingly agreed.

THE INSPECTOR'S TRAGIC END

Wang Shenhan threw a lavish banquet in honour of Li Yuchang's arrival, which Li was obliged to attend in conformity with etiquette. Bowing and scraping, Wang plied Li with quantities of food and wine. When he returned to his provisional residence, the thirsty inspector drank a cup of hot tea to which Li Xiang had added a draught of arsenic. Before long the poison was causing Li Yuchang stabbing pains in the stomach. His heartless servants, Li Xiang, Gu Xiang and Ma Liansheng, rushed into his bedroom at this moment and pinned their master to the floor. "I just want to tell you," said Li Xiang, grinning, "that we've had it up to here serving you." Then Ma Liansheng tied a rope around Li Yuchang's neck and strangled him to death. To cover their deed, the three servants hanged his body from a beam, making it look like the inspector had committed suicide.

The next day it was announced that Li Yuchang had hanged himself. Believing that their plot had come off without a hitch, Wang Shenhan ordered Bao Xiang and three servants to clean up the scene of the crime and eliminate all possible evidence. He then rushed to Huai'an Prefecture to report the incident.

The Huai'an prefect, Wang Gu, was a greedy official who often winked at Wang Shenhan's misbehaviour if only because the latter had bribed him. Coming straight to the point, Wang Shenhan told him the entire story of Li Yuchang's death and made him an offer of 2,000 taels of silver, hoping Wang Gu would do something on his behalf. At first, Wang hesitated because he knew the possible consequences of complying with the magistrate's request — it was, after all, a provincially appointed inspector that was involved in the case. Finally, however, his greed got the best of him.

Back in his office, Wang Shenhan spooned out silver to all his subordinates and advised them to mind their own business. He then ordered a coroner's inquest. Traces of strangling around the neck and a purplish tinge in the face suggested death by hanging, he said at first. But he faltered in his conclusion a minute later, when he saw signs of bleeding from the mouth and nose and observed the victim's darkened fingernails, all of which suggested poisoning. Unable to determine the true cause of Li Yuchang's death, the coroner proposed a test with a silver probe. At this point, the prefect flew into a rage and ordered that the coroner be caned for his "incompetence and contradictory statements". This left him with little choice but to file a report that Li Yuchang had hanged himself. The prefect more than readily "approved" this conclusion and ordered the body to be sealed in a coffin. He then wound up the case by submitting a report of his own version of the case to the higher authorities.

A COMPLAINT OF INJUSTICE

The credulous provincial judge and treasurer raised no objections to the report from the Huai'an prefect. Nor did the Governor-General of Jiangsu, Jiangxi and Anhui investigate the case any further before declaring it closed.

With these details taken care of, Wang Shenhan notified Li Yuchang's family to come for the coffin and prepare for the funeral. Meanwhile, he recommended Li Xiang to become the runner of a friend of his who was a district official in charge of grain transport and farmland improvements, secured a lucrative position for Ma Liansheng in a neighbouring county, and gave a handsome sum of money to Gu Xiang, who chose to return to his native village.

It appeared as if the case of Li Yuchang's death was closed forever, but the march of events took a sudden turn when early in the fourteenth year of the Jiaqing, an uncle of Li Yuchang arrived in Shanyang County to take away his nephew's corpse and personal belongings. In Li Yuchang's manuscripts, he found a page bearing these lines: "The Shanyang County magistrate made fraudulent claims concerning the relief funds. He tried to bribe me, hoping that I would shield him, but I refused." This aroused Li Taiqing's suspicion about his nephew's death, but since he lacked any definitive evidence to challenge the coroner's verdict, he could do nothing at the time. He accepted the 150 taels of silver issued by the magistrate as funeral expenses, and escorted the coffin home.

While carrying out the preparations for the funeral, Li Yuchang's widow found a blood-stained coat among her late husband's belongings. She reported this to Li Taiqing, who was even more suspicious now about the real cause of Yuchang's death. At his urging, the family decided to open the coffin and examine Li Yuchang's body. They found that his fingernails were all black and blue, and when they inserted a silver hair-pin into his throat, the metal darkened, a clear sign of poisoning. Li Taiqing then travelled to the imperial capital to lodge a complaint with the Metropolitan Censorate, which reported the case to the throne.

THE EMPEROR ENRAGED

Well aware that one method of saving the rapidly declining Qing Dynasty was for the government to commend loyal officials and punish corrupt ones, Emperor Jiaqing paid particular attention to Li Taiqing's written complaint. Having read it carefully, he issued an edict to the Grand Council, pointing out that "the cause of Li Yuchang's death is highly suspicious. There very likely has been a miscarriage of justice in the handling of this case. All possible wrongs must be redressed."

He also queried, "Why would Li Yuchang want to commit suicide after returning from the banquet? Why did Wang Shenhan go to the trouble of making comfortable arrangements for Li Xiang and other servants of Li Yuchang? Since the case involves suspicions about the death of an imperial official," stressed the emperor, "a thorough investigation is called for so." He ordered that Li Yuchang's corpse be brought to the provincial capital for a thorough examination, and that the Shanyang magistrate and the other persons involved be summoned to the imperial capital to be interrogated by the Grand Council with the co-operation of the Board of Punishments.

When the corpse was brought before a group of experienced coroners for the second inquest, it was already in a state of decay. An examination of the bones revealed that they were all black and blue except for the ribcage, which remained dark yellow. The coroners concluded that the dark colour of the bones indicated arsenic poisoning, and that the condition of the ribcage suggested that Li Yuchang had died of other causes before his vital organs were overcome by the effects of the poison.

In Beijing, the Grand Councillors and officials of the Board of Punishments cross-examined Wang Shenhan, Bao Xiang, Li Xiang, Gu Xiang and Ma Liansheng, all of whom pleaded guilty in face of the irrefutable evidence. Their confessions corroborated one another, so that a clear picture of the case emerged.

These results were reported to the throne without delay. In the meantime, the Governor-General of Jiangsu, Jiangxi and Anhui also sent a memorial to the emperor in which he stated that he had suspected poisoning, and that he had questioned those present at the banquet and the cooks responsible for preparing the dishes that day. "But all to no avail," the Governor-General continued, "so that Li Yuchang's case remains unsettled." This memorial infuriated Emperor Jiaqing, who had the Governor-General dismissed from office and banished to the border province of Xinjiang for his "intolerable muddle-headedness which disqualifies him from acting as the head of three provinces".

THE CRIMINALS PUNISHED

It took six months to close the case, during which time Emperor Jiaqing took a personal interest in it, reading the relevant documents and issuing the necessary instructions. When all became clear, the throne decreed that Li Yuchang be posthumously promoted to the position of prefect and cited him as "an example of how imperial officials should perform their duties". A grand funeral ceremony was held for the late relief fund inspector who was "a paragon of honesty". Moreover, the emperor composed a sixty-line poem in praise of Li, the text of which was inscribed on a fine stone tablet placed in front of Li Yuchang's tomb. Li's uncle, Li Taiqing, received the title of "successful provincial candidate in the imperial martial arts examination". Since Li Yuchang was childless, Emperor Jiaqing chose an heir for him; the adopted son, too, received the title of "successful provincial candidate".

Wang Shenhan was decapitated and his family's property confiscated for "embezzling relief funds and poisoning an honest inspector who was above accepting

The sleeping chambers of the Ming and Qing empresses.

An imperial concubine of Emperor Yongzhen.

乾隆元年八月吉日

Emperor Qianlong in September 1736, the first year of his 60-year reign.

Emperor Qianlong, painted by a Roman Catholic priest.

Qianqinggong (Hall of Heavenly Purity) where the emperors and Empress Dowagers Cixi and Ci'an receive their ministers.

Empress Dowager Cixi in her sixties.

The reform-minded Emperor Guangxu.

bribes from him". In addition, since Wang's brutality "not only led to the death of Li Yuchang but also broke the latter's family line", Wang's sons were exiled to the border region of Yili in Xinjiang "in revenge".

Wang Gu, the Huai'an prefect who "abused power by shielding a culprit, taking bribes, and colluding with a criminal", was sentenced to hanging.

For helping his master murder Li Yuchang, Bao Xiang was also beheaded, while Li's servants, Li Xiang, Gu Xiang and Ma Liansheng, were sentenced to "slow death by dismemberment". However, for acting as "the principal culprit in the murder case", Li Xiang was escorted to Li Yuchang's tomb to be executed and "have his heart cut out to dispell public indignation".

ARMED REBELS STORM
THE FORBIDDEN CITY

Feng Zuozhe and Li Shangying

In the autumn of 1813, the Qing imperial palace became the scene of a bloody battle when about one hundred armed rebels, believers in the Heavenly Principle Sect, raided the nerve Forbidden City.

This took place during the Jiaqing reign (1796-1820), when the outwardly prosperous Qing empire was beginning to show signs of decline: excessive concentration of land in the hands of a minority and political corruption, which, coupled with recurrent natural disasters and the resulting misery of the people, further aggravated social instability and gave rise to successive peasant revolts.

Although the imperial capital of Beijing was regarded as "the showplace" of the Qing Dynasty, its residents fared no better than Chinese people elsewhere because of political oppression and economic exploitation. Historical records reveal that "scores of kilometres away from Beijing proper, people lived in rude huts and ate coarse beans. They were as impoverished as those who lived in remote, backward areas." The peasants "lived from hand to mouth, and life became impossible whenever natural calamities struck". In the latter part of the Jiaqing reign, serious drought was reported in Beijing and the three provinces of Zhili (now Hebei), Shandong and Henan. Only some 15 kilogrammes of grain were harvested from each *mu** of land. Hunger and cold drove large numbers of peasants to join the secret Heavenly Principle Sect and its armed struggle to topple the Qing regime. The raid on the imperial palace which took place on the 15th day of the ninth month of the 18th year of the Jiaqing reign (1813) was a major expression of this anti-Qing cause.

Active chiefly in suburban Beijing and Zhili, Henan and Shandong provinces, the Heavenly Principle Sect was organized by Lin Qing (in Beijing), Li Wencheng (in Henan) and Feng Keshan (in Shandong). To realize its ultimate objective, the organization preached its doctines in an attempt to recruit as many members as possible. In 1811, the sect's three leaders met clandestinely and worked out a plan for an uprising to be held in the autumn of 1813. Lin was to seize Beijing, Li occupy Henan and Feng take Shandong. As Lin stormed into the Forbidden City and took over the capital, the other two were to lead their men on a northward march. As that was when Emperor Jiaqing customarily went to Rehe on his hunting trips, the three columns of peasant rebels planned to ambush the sovereign on his return to Beijing. Thus, they calculated, they would be able to drive the Manchus back to the northeast and overthrow the Qing Dynasty.

---

* One *mu* equals one-fifteenth of a hectare

Lin Qing prepared for the armed uprising by ordering his disciple Li Wu to make swords and spears in
Gu'an County, Zhili Province, and selected more than
two hundred strong men from various counties near
Beijing to be trained as the core insurrectionary force.
To mould public opinion in favour of his future action,
Lin composed a folksong with the theme, "Put Lin Qing
on the throne and wheat flour will be cheap." He allied
himself with court eunuchs who could help his men
take the imperial palace. As early as 1801 Lin had
opened a shop which sold quails not far from the Forbidden City, a front through which he made the acquaintance of some low-ranking eunuchs and won them
over to his religion, whose main tenets could be boiled
down to two statements: "The world of the senses is
a void. Being comes from non-being." Liu Decai, the
first eunuch to be converted to the sect, won over
several other eunuchs to Lin Qing's sect. Later they
acted from within the palace walls in co-ordination
with the rebels attacking from without.

One month before the date set for the uprising, Lin
Qing and the other leaders held a meeting to discuss
their final arrangements. They selected a white banner
bearing the words "Spread the doctrine according to
heavenly mandate", as their official flag, and the words
"*desheng*" meaning "victory" as their secret password.
The two hundred armed men would be organized into
small detachments of ten or twelve soldiers, each with
its own leader and a white banner. To identify themselves, the rebels would wear around their waists white
cloths bearing the words, "Of one heart and one mind,
we stand firmly together", and a white turban with
words "Peace throughout the year". For the actual at-

tack, the armed peasants were to charge into the palace from the Eastern Flowery Gate and the Western Flowery Gate. The eastern group would be commanded by Chen Shuang, with Liu Chengxiang bringing up the rear, and with the eunuchs Liu Decai and Liu Jin acting as guides. The western group was to be led by Chen Wenkui, with Liu Yongtai bringing up the rear and the eunuchs Yang Jinzhong, Gao Guangfu and Zhang Tai acting as guides. Chen Shuang was appointed general commander of the assault force, and the eunuch Wang Fulu was to act from within the Forbidden City.

On the 14th day of the ninth month, Chen Shuang and Chen Wenkui led a section of their men into Beijing and found lodgings outside the Yongdingmen Gate and the Front Gate (both are in the south of Tiananmen Gate behind which is the Forbidden City). The next morning, more peasant rebels entered the city. Although this was the day of the planned uprising, only 100 men had arrived, the rest having not been notified in time or having failed to arrive according to schedule. These hundred men were divided into two groups. Most of them were disguised as pedlars carrying baskets in which their swords and daggers were concealed.

In the middle of the afternoon, the eastern group arrived outside the Eastern Flowery Gate. One of the peasant rebels started a quarrel with a coolie transporting coal into the Forbidden City. Without thinking, the former took off his jacket, ready to fight, but the coolie, spotting a dagger concealed on his opponent, shouted for help. This alerted the nearby palace guards who rushed to shut the gate. At that critical moment, the rebels took out their weapons and charged into the palace. But only half a dozen of them, including Chen

Shuang, succeeded in forcing their way through the gate. The majority, including Liu Chengxiang, had to disperse and flee. Aided by the eunuchs Liu Decai and Liu Jin, Chen Shuang and the others advanced to the Gate of Harmony where they engaged the palace guards in a skirmish. Gioro Baoxing, Vice-Minister of the Board of Rites, ordered the closing of the Gate of Flourishing Fortune, one of the main gates in the central section of the Forbidden City, and then rushed to report the incident to Minning, the second son of the reigning sovereign and the future Emperor Daoguang (reigned 1821-1850). Minning grabbed a shotgun and a heavy knife, prepared for a show-down with the attackers.

Meanwhile, the western group consisting of about 50 men broke into the Forbidden City with the help of the eunuch Yang Jinzhong. They closed the Western Flowery Gate and climbed onto the gatetower where they hoisted the white banner. A number of them headed towards the Hall of Mental Cultivation, the emperor's private apartments. Waving banners inscribed with "The Great Ming Dynasty — a Heavenly Mandate" and "Obey the Heavenly Mandate, Protect the Populace" and guided by the eunuch Gao Guangfu, they reached the Gate of Imperial Prosperity, which had been closed. Others headed for the Hall of Literary Treasures and the Imperial Clothing Storage, outside which they fought hand-to-hand against the palace guards.

Though they had been caught unawares, Minning and a few other princes quickly came out to resist the rebels. They gained confidence after Minning had shot down two attackers from the stone steps in front of the Hall of Mental Cultivation. Zhaolian, Prince Li and Mianke, Prince Zhuang brought in more than 1,000 imperial troops who were to be sent to Henan to suppress Li Wencheng's revolt. Mianke, Prince Zhuang led about 100 of them and scores of spear-armed soldiers to the Gate of Imperial Prosperity, to which General Yulin was also hurrying with some of his own men. In the fierce battle there, several of the outnumbered rebels were killed or arrested, while the rest retreated south only to find that their planned escape route, the Western Flowery Gate, was blocked. At this time, Gao Guangfu led the rebels onto the palace walls where was seen waving a banner bearing the words "The Great Ming Dynasty — a Heavenly Mandate". Gao was struck by an arrow shot by Yihac, Duke of National Defence (Zhenguo) and fell off the gatetower. At this point, a mason working in the palace guided a leading rebel, Li Wu, and others concealed among the stone couches. A few of the remaining rebels escaped by jumping over the vermilion walls, but most of them continued fighting at the Palace of Benevolent Peace, the Five-Phoenix Tower and the Hall of the South Wind.

In direct contrast to the valour of the insurrectionists was the cowardice of the Qing rulers. The imperial consorts, princes, ministers and generals might act in an overweening manner towards the populace, but the rebellious peasant attack made them as nervous as birds; most of them were ready to show a clean pair of heels to save their skin. Both the commander of the imperial guards, Shi Ruiling, Prince Li, and Zhaolian, ordered carriages to be readied for the empress and imperial concubines to flee Beijing. Celing, a Mongol general in charge of the Meridian Gate, fled on foot at the head of a group of his men when word of the raid reached him. Days after the incident, all the inhabitants of the Forbidden City turned pale at the mere mention of it. The emperor ordered his eunuchs to take specially prepared medicines to relieve them of their "mental uneasiness" and to drive away the "evil spirits" possessing them.

Two days after the attack, the Qing authorities began searching for peasant insurrectionists in the capital, and more than thirty were arrested. The principal leader Lin Qing, who had been directing the struggle from a village outside Beijing, fell into the hands of the imperial soldiers when somebody informed on him.

Emperor Jiaqing, who had been in his Rehe Mountain Resort, broke off his autumn hunting trip at nearby Mulan and rushed back to Beijing when he received the report of the attack. He made a gesture of "self-criticism" while stating in great anger, "In sending his evil followers to harass the Forbidden City against the interests of the state, Lin Qing has committed a towering crime." Troops were dispatched to comb the rebels' base of operations in suburban Daxing County, arrest the remaining rebels and set fire to their headquarters. Orders were given that "no stones be left unturned in trying the criminals, all of them should be disposed of and any possible source of future trouble uprooted". A week after this, Emperor Jiaqing personally interrogated Lin Qing, Liu Decai and Liu Jin before having them executed. Other insurrectionists who had been arrested were subjected to more than 40 days of interrogation and ruthless torture, after which they and their family members were sentenced to slow death by dismemberment and subsequent beheading, simple beheading, hanging, flogging, forced labour, or exile. Some of their ancestral graves were opened and the occupants exhumed and "beheaded".

To stave off further trouble, the Qing government planted detectives throughout the country, strengthened the "neighbourhood guarantee" (*baojia*) system, burned books "preaching evil-doing", tightened control over the eunuchs and the members of the imperial household, increased checkpoints along the major roads and improved training in the army. Despite these measures, many important members of the Heavenly Principle Sect were not caught for many years. For example, Liu Chengxiang, Zhu Xian, Li Diwu, Dong Bowang, Zhi Jincai and Liu Chengzhang, all whom the Qing authorities had been trying to arrest, remained at large up to the Daoguang reign (1821-1850).

The Heavenly Principle uprising though unsuccessful left its mark on the history of popular anti-Qing struggle. In the words of a Qing scholar, "The incident fully exposed the laxity and corruption of the imperial government, the stupidity of Qing officialdom, the unpopularity of the imperial rule, and the declining capacity of the Qing army."

THE "VIRTUOUS IMPERIAL CONCUBINE" BEARS A SON

Liu Guilin

Among the huge corpus of written records now preserved in the Palace Museum in Beijing, two volumes
of data are on the pregnancy and maternity of many
Qing Dynasty court ladies, one of whom was a Virtuous
Imperial Concubine, better known to the world after
the death of Emperor Xianfeng (reigned 1850-1861)
as Empress Dowager Cixi. A description of how this
concubine of Emperor Xianfeng was cared for during
the months before she gave birth to the boy who reveals
curious details about life in the imperial family at the
time.

According to the rules of the imperial household,
when an imperial concubine became pregnant, one of
the members of her own family was allowed to enter
the palace to look after her. In the twelfth month of
the fifth year of Xianfeng's reign, the Virtuous Imperial
Concubine, who at this point had been pregnant for six
months, was beginning having difficulty getting about.
On the twenty-fourth of the same month, the chief

eunuch Han Laiyu transmitted an imperial rescript permitting the Virtuous Concubine's mother to come and stay in the Palace of Concentrated Beauty. Two weeks after the lunar New Year celebration, the Imperial Court Affairs Department brought 30 maids to the Virtuous Concubine's, from among whom she selected six, two to handle important responsibilities and four to perform ordinary tasks. They began attending the pregnant imperial consort approximately one week later. The day they began their work, two midwives and two imperial physicians were recruited for round-the-clock service. And before long, another four physicians were appointed, so that the six of them could look after the expectant Virtuous Concubine in two shifts.

Meanwhile, all the necessary clothing and equipment were being readied. On the third day of the second month, the clothing section of the Imperial Court Affairs Department was ordered to purchase 75.1 *chi* of coloured pongee, 81.3 *chi* of coloured Lu'an silk, three bolts of white Korean cotton, three bolts of blue Korean cotton, two bolts of bleached white cotton, and two bolts of blue homespun. This fabric was used to make 27 jackets (18 cotton-padded and 9 lined), four short gowns, 75 bedsheets of varying sizes, four stomachers, two makeshift curtains, 18 quilts, 12 mattresses of varying sizes, two bags filled with bran, four bands, and one door curtain. At the same time, the general affairs section was notified to prepare two wooden tubs, two wooden bowls, one wooden shovel and one small wooden knife. Two days later, on the fifth of the same month, the provisions section was ordered to procure a black felt blanket 6×4 *chi* and an "auspicious" cradle. On the ninth day of the third month, one of the doctors requested a "childbirth-hastening" stone. On the 13th, all the items listed above were delivered to the Palace of Concentrated Beauty for the Virtuous Imperial Concubine to examine. On the 19th, the chief eunuch obtained a sword from the Palace of Mental Cultivation, which was then hung in the rear hall of the Palace of Concentrated Beauty for the purpose of frightening away evil spirits.

From the very first day he learned of the Virtuous Concubine's conception, Emperor Xianfeng paid the closest attention to her health. From the third day of the second month, the imperial physicians and midwives were told to attend her day and night. His Majesty demanded timely reports on her appetite and her sleep as well as on the performance of those who were caring for her. He was particularly concerned with the condition of her pulse and the development of the foetus. On the 24th day of the first month, imperial physicians Luan Tai, Li Wanqing, Ying Wenxi and Kuang Mao-zhong reported that the Virtuous Concubine's pulse beat was regular, and that this indicated normal growth. One month later, in the eighth month of pregnancy, the physicians reported the same thing. On the ninth day of the third month, they assured the emperor that her condition was stable as she entered her ninth month. The next day, the midwives examined her and estimated that childbirth would occur some time between the end of the third month and the beginning of the fourth. The throne was naturally extremely glad to learn all of this.

Earlier, specifically at noon on the 24th day of the first month, three eunuchs from the construction section of the Imperial Court Affairs Department dug a small "Pit of Great Happiness" behind the Palace of Concentrated Beauty for the purpose of burying the after-birth and other objects discarded during this period. When the digging was finished, two midwives chanted "songs of good luck" as they threw into the pit chopsticks (*kuaizi* in Chinese, a pun on "smooth delivery of an infant boy"), scarlet silk and gold and silver ingots.

A little past nine o'clock on the morning of the 23rd day of the third month in the sixth year of Xianfeng's reign, the Virtuous Concubine began to feel increasingly ill. The midwives concluded that this was a sign of impending childbirth, and the chief eunuch hastened to report this to the throne. A son was delivered some time after one o'clock in the afternoon of the same day. Both mother and infant were in excellent health.

According to the "Imperial Household Regulations", an imperial concubine of the Virtuous Concubine's status would be presented with 200 taels of silver and 40 bolts of fine dress material a dozen days after bearing a child. On the fifth day of the fourth month, when the chief eunuch asked the throne to do this, Xianfeng responded without delay — but only after having promulgated a rescript which announced in vermilion letters the promotion of the Virtuous Concubine by one rank. She was awarded 300 taels of silver and 70 bolts of first-class fabric as a result.

EMPEROR XIANFENG DIES IN HIS SUMMER RESORT

Rong Shidi

Chengde, some 250 kilometres northeast of Beijing, is the location of the Qing Imperial Summer Mountain Resort, built between 1703 and 1790. Within its grounds stands the Hall of Misty Scenery and Pleasant Coolness. Noted for its simple style — the building is constructed of unpainted wood with blue roof tiles — much of its elegance is derived from the ancient pines and cypresses which grow in front of it. The hall was the place where the Qing emperors received their empresses and concubines. One room was used as a temple where the sovereigns offered Buddhist prayers every morning. An inner room, the Western Warm Chamber, was the emperor's private apartment, and was decorated with precious ceramics, jade carvings, paintings and calligraphy. To the south stood a low cushioned couch covered with dragon-patterned silk of imperial yellow and a small golden-lacquered table displaying the emperor's writing implements. To the north side of the room stood the imperial "dragon bed" with its sky-blue curtains, yellow spread and quilts of damask silk. It was on this bed that the seventh Qing emperor, Xianfeng (reigned 1851-1861), passed away early on the morning of the 17th day of the seventh month in the 11th year of his reign, at the age of thirty-one.

Fleeing from the Anglo-French forces which had invaded Beijing, Xianfeng arrived at the Chengde summer resort on the 16th day of the eight month in the previous year (September 20, 1860), his retinue including his empress and imperial concubine who after his death became Empress Dowager Ci'an and Empress Dowager Cixi, eleven concubines and his five-year-old son Zaichun.

Regarding the cause of Xianfeng's death, an imperial decree issued soon afterwards in the name of the succeeding boy emperor (reign title Tongzhi) stated, "His Majesty suffered from coughing in the summer of last year. But it was quickly cured. He was in good health when he went to Chengde on an inspection tour last autumn. He worked hard day and night handling local rebellions. He caught a cold this spring, which caused a relapse of his old illness. Diarrhoea in the sixth month expended his vital energy, and his condition seriously worsened on the 16th day of the seventh month. He passed away at the *yin* hour (3:00 to 5:00 a.m.) of the 17th."

As a matter of fact, "working hard day and night" was not exaggerated praise. For, when he ascended the throne at the age of twenty, the empire Xianfeng inherited from Emperor Daoguang was in a dreadful state. The year of his enthronement, 1851, saw the outbreak of the Taiping Revolution. The imperial army suffered successive defeats at the hands of the peasant revolutionaries, causing increasing worry for Emperor Xianfeng and exacerbating his capriciousness. Then came the Second Opium War (1856-1860) during which foreign troops invaded Beijing and set fire to his favourite Yuanmingyuan (Old Summer Palace). Domestic troubles and foreign aggression "added to his mental burden and consumed his vital energy". Moreover, having been spoilt by a life of debauchery since childhood, his constitution was poor to begin with. He became increasingly susceptible to disease, and the winter cold of Chengde was too much for him.

Emperor Xianfeng's old illness recurred in the spring of the 11th year of his reign with such added force that he decided to return to Beijing. He told his ministers, "I cough more and more often, spitting phlegm with traces of blood. I need a good rest." But he did not go back to the capital. Whenever he recovered slightly, he sought further indulgence with his concubines. Summer came, and he was still in poor health. Then he suffered diarrhoea early in June of the same year. On the ninth of the month he recovered sufficiently to receive his ministers who gathered to celebrate his 31st birthday. In the middle of a birthday banquet, he suddenly took sick and had to return to his bed-chamber, supported by eunuchs. That was his last public appearance. The medicine prescribed by the best imperial physicians was of no help. By midnight of the 16th day, he knew his end was near. Summoning to his presence the leading officials of the Department of Imperial Household Affairs and his eight senior Grand Councillors — Sushun, Zaiyuan, Duanhua, Jingshou, Muyin, Kuangyuan, Du Han and Jiao Youying

— he drafted his will, naming his only son, Aisin-Gioro Zaichun to be his successor. He told the eight Grand Councillors, "Exert yourselves in assisting the new emperor in the administration of state affairs." Early the next morning he breathed his last. Zaichun, six years of age, assumed the title of emperor.

Events developed apace following Emperor Xianfeng's death. In collusion with Prince Gong (1833-1898), Empress Dowager Cixi, mother of the newly installed Emperor Tongzhi, staged a palace coup, wresting supreme power from the eight Grand Councillors who were later either executed or banished to remote regions. Beginning in late 1861, Cixi began her regency, attending to affairs of court from behind a screen while the boy emperor sat on the throne. The series of events which led up to this came to be known as the "Coup of 1861".

YANG NAIWU AND "LITTLE CABBAGE"

Jin Jin

For several generations, the story *Yang Naiwu and Little Cabbage* has been performed on China's stages in dozens of dramatic forms. It is also a favourite item in the repertoire of story-tellers and ballad singers. Its complicated, suspenseful plot is based on a frame-up case that took place in the late Qing Dynasty. The details of the incidents upon which the popular tale is based are to be found among the archives of the Qing Board of Punishments in the Palace Museum in Beijing.

HONEST SCHOLAR AND PRETTY TENANT

Yang Naiwu was a scholar from Yuhang County (in the north of Hangzhou City), Zhejiang Province who became a *juren* (a successful provincial candidate in the imperial examinations) in 1873. "Little Cabbage" was the nickname of a delicate and pretty young woman Bi Xiugu, the wife of Ge Pinlian, a bean curd maker from the Yuhang county seat. She was so nicknamed for always wearing green jade clothing with a white apron.

Because of mounting discord between his wife and mother, Ge Pinlian rented a room from Yang Naiwu and moved in with Little Cabbage to get away from the old woman. Yang and his tenants got along well at first. But what with narrow-minded Ge Pinlian, who suspected illicit relations between his pretty wife and the newly widowed scholar landlord, and Ge Pinlian's wicked, inquisitive mother, who was a habitual gossip-monger, Yang found it increasingly difficult to live in the same courtyard with them.

Before long, rumours of an affair between Yang and Little Cabbage spread quickly. It soon became the talk of the town, and the scholar was forced to raise the rent by a big percentage as a way of driving Ge Pinlian and his wife out of his courtyard. Ge Pinlian, who correctly understood Yang's move, was only too glad to leave. This took place in the summer of 1873, the 12th year of the Tongzhi period.

That should have been the end of the affair. But, due to the corruption of the county magistrate and the incompetence of the coroner, Yang Naiwu and Little Cabbage were soon imprisoned on a frame-up. Luckily for them strife between two cliques of Qing officials saved their lives in an odd turn of events.

Ge Pinlian had always been in poor health, and on the seventh day of the tenth month of 1873, he had a serious relapse. Too weak to work, he returned home from his shop two days later. On the night of the ninth, he turned in earlier than usual, and about midnight, Little Cabbage discovered foam issuing from his mouth. Ge Pinlian's mother arrived early the next morning and sent for a doctor, who diagnosed "eruptive disease". Failing to respond to medicine, the patient died the same day.

Though she found nothing abnormal about her son's death, the vicious old woman, who never liked her daughter-in-law in the first place, now recalled the so-called "affair" between the widow and Yang Naiwu and hit upon the idea of accusing Little Cabbage of murdering her son. She had a scribe write a complaint for her and then brought a charge against the young woman to the county *yamen*.

The magistrate of Yuhang County, Liu Xitong, had a long official career and was highly regarded of by his superiors and colleagues. Although the written complaint submitted by Little Cabbage's mother-in-law contained no direct reference to Yang Naiwu, he knew whom the old woman was after, since he had learned through hearsay of the "illicit relations" between Yang and Little Cabbage. Accompanied by a coroner and a number of *yamen* runners, he proceeded to the Ge family to investigate, intending to make a display of his competence and reap personal gain.

As the autumn weather in southern China was still rather hot, Ge Pinlian's corpse had begun to rot, and the light-coloured liquid oozing from his mouth and nose had spread about his ears and eyes. The coroner, Shen Xiang, who knew nothing of his profession and was utterly irresponsible, incorrectly diagnosed this condition as "bleeding from the seven apertures". Seeing that Ge Pinlian's fingernails had darkened (as a matter of fact, this was due to excessive loss of blood), Shen Xiang placed a silver probe in his mouth once and examined it without repeating the test. Its dull colour led him to conclude that Ge Pinlian had been poisoned. When asked what the poison was, Shen Xiang replied without much thinking, "It's opium." A runner beside him chimed in, "Death by swallowing opium is impossible in Ge Pinlian's case. He must have died from arsenic poisoning." The verdict of "poisoning" was just what the eccentric magistrate was waiting for, and he hurried back to his *yamen* and had Little Cabbage brought to the court for trial.

Verbal abuse coupled with torture made the young woman plead guilty to murdering her husband in collusion with the "adulterer" Yang Naiwu, who, she said, had provided her with the arsenic.

FROM BRIDAL CHAMBER TO PRISON

At that time, Yang Naiwu had just passed the provincial imperial examinations and was attending his wedding ceremony. Little did he expect that at this very moment he would be dragged off to the county court. At first he refused to admit any guilt, but cruel and repeated torture forced him to make the confession the magistrate wanted to hear and Yang was cast also into prison.

Yang confessed that he had procured arsenic from a druggist named Qian Baosheng — a name he made up under pressure — when he told him that the poison was going to be used to kill rats in his home. The only druggist in the county town whose surname was Qian was summoned to court, but he explained that his personal name was "Tan" rather than "Baosheng". Anxious to close the case, the magistrate promised him that he would be set free only if he were willing to co-operate.

Qian hesitated. At this juncture, the druggist's younger brother Qian Kai asked a good friend of the magistrate, a scholar named Chen Zhushan, to intercede on his brother's behalf. Jealous of Yang Naiwu's academic achievements, Chen "hit a man when he was down" and offered testimony on behalf of the druggist, who then committed perjury to save his own skin. The court sentenced Little Cabbage to slow death by dismemberment, and Yang Naiwu to beheading. Before reporting the case to the higher authorities for approval, the magistrate told his men to patch up any contradictory statements. In this way they managed to deceive the prefectual and provincial authorities, and thus the case was transmitted to the Board of Punishments in Beijing for final examination.

Unreconciled to the sentence imposed on him, Yang Naiwu drafted a statement of self-defence and asked his sister to present it to the imperial Censorate in Beijing. Meanwhile, his new wife sought out friends to help her lodge a complaint with the prefectural military authorities.

At this time the Qing empire was in decline and corruption was widespread. Miscarriages of justice were so common that even the imperial officials admitted that not even one in a hundred mishandled cases which the central authorities instructed the local courts to re-examine had a chance of being redressed. Arbitrary decisions, flattery, partiality, mutual protection and collusion on the part of judicial personnel made a reversal of Yang Naiwu and Little Cabbage's convictions well-nigh impossible. Yet a strange combination of factors brought about a dramatic turn in their favour and created a great stir throughout the capital.

When the Censorate in Beijing received the written complaints from Yang Naiwu and his second wife, it ordered the Zhejiang governor Yang Changjun (?-1897) to look into the case. The governor, who had originally approved the judgement, now felt he had to go through the motions of instructing the Hangzhou prefecture to conduct a new investigation. The Hangzhou prefect and the Yuhang magistrate both reported back perfunctorily that no injustice had been done in the case under review. These Zhejiang mandarins never expected that word would eventually leak out about the trumped-up case.

What counted the most in such cases was, of course, politics. In the strife raging among the various cliques in those days, the Zhejiang group had expanded so fast that it had wrested a great deal of military power in the region. Naturally it became the target of other coteries and even Empress Dowager Cixi, who while "attending to state affairs from behind a screen" began to regard it as a threat. Cixi's followers were quick to seize on Yang Naiwu's case and make an issue of it. In the fourth months of the first year of Emperor Guang-xu's reign (1875-1908), a supervisory official named Wang Shurui memorialized the throne and criticized the Zhejiang governor Yang Changjun for shielding his subordinates in the handling of the Yang Naiwu case. The Empress Dowager decreed that the Zhejiang provincial literary chancellor, Hu Ruilan, review the case. Working hand in glove with Yang Changjun, however, Hu subjected Yang Naiwu and Little Cabbage to interrogation and torture for several days, and the two victims, who had both withdrawn their confessions at an earlier trial, yielded once again. Hu Ruilan reported back to Beijing, enormously proud of the "clean government" in his province. It never occurred to him that, six months later, an imperial censor named Bian Baoquan would venture to submit a memorial of his own to Emperor Guangxu and the Empress Dowager exposing the dirty deal between Yang Changjun and Hu Ruilan and proposing that the Board of Punishments intervene directly. Bian Baoquan's proposal was accepted.

The Minister of Punishments, Zaobao, took personal charge of the matter. After carefully reading through the files, trying the "culprits" and examining the personal testimonies, he raised a number of queries which he thought could only be solved by a second autopsy of Ge Pinlian's corpse. Thus, three years after burial the dead body was brought to Beijing from Yuhang County on the ninth day of the 12th month of the second year of Guangxu's reign. The new inquest, made in the presence of Zaobao and his assistants, the Yuhang magistrate Liu Xitong, coroner Shen Xiang, Little Cabbage and her mother-in-law, revealed no signs of poisoning. Completely disarmed, Liu and Shen pleaded guilty. Yang Naiwu and Little Cabbage were declared innocent and set free.

This was a chance for the Empress Dowager to do away with some wildly ambitious Zhejiang officials and reduce the strength of the local clique, all in the name of benefiting the populace. The Zhejiang governor Yang Changjun, provincial literary chancellor Hu Ruilan, the Hangzhou prefect Chen Lu and scores of other local officials were deprived of their official ranks and severely punished. As for the others involved, the Yuhang magistrate was banished to the remote northeastern province of Heilongjiang, coroner Shen was sentenced to two years' imprisonment after receiving eighty strokes of the bamboo, while Little Cabbage's mother-in-law and the druggist Qian Tan received their due punishments.

EMPRESS DOWAGER CIXI'S TRAIN TRIP TO THE WESTERN TOMBS

Wu Fei

Nine of the ten Qing emperors, who ruled China from 1644 to 1911, were all buried in Hebei Province. Their burial sites, known as the Eastern and Western Tombs, are located in two beautiful mountain settings some one-hundred kilometres to the east and west of Beijing. Whenever the reigning emperor paid his respects to his predecessors, he was accompanied on his journey by a vast retinue. Imperial sedan chairs, horses, carts and attendants and armed guards carrying colourful banners and glistening weapons stretched in a line kilometres long. Bringing up the rear was a contingent of servants transporting everything from sacrificial vessels, rare delicacies and other foodstuffs, everyday articles and cooking utensils right down to drinking water and medicine. Journeys on this scale naturally meant an enormous expenditure of human, financial and material resources, the burden of which lay on the shoulders of the common people.

110

Empress Dowager Cixi's journey by train to the Western Tombs in 1903, the 29th year of Emperor Guangxu's reign, seemed a much more economical way to go. The facts, however, show that this was but another means — modern means at that — of squandering national wealth. According to historical records, two short railway lines were built specially for the Empress Dowager's trip; one leading southwest from Beijing to Lugouqiao (the Marco Polo Bridge), and the other from Gaobeidian to Yixian County, Hebei Province, leading right up to the Tailing, the burial place of Emperor Yongzheng (reigned 1723-1735). Sheng Xuanhuai, Vice-Minister of Commerce, and Yuan Shikai, Governor-General of Zhili (now Hebei) and concurrently Minister of Foreign Trade for Northern Coastal Provinces, were ordered to take joint charge of the construction of these railways, which were in fact extensions of the Lugouqiao-Hankou line.

For some details about the Gaobeidian-Yixian Railway, we shall quote from a memorial by Yuan Shikai to the throne contained in *A Sequel to the "Annals of the Qing Dynasty"*: "Your humble subject went on an inspection tour of the Gaobeidian-Yixian Railway by first travelling by train to its starting point in Xincheng County. He carefully inspected the entire line to its conclusion at Liangguzhuang in Yixian. The distance between Gaobeidian and Laishui is 27 *li* (1 *li* = 0.5 km.), that between Laishui and the Yixian county seat 34 *li*, and that between the county seat and Lianggezhuang 17 *li*, making a total of 78 *li*. Stations have been built at each of these places, all on level ground. The railway bridges are sturdy structures. . . . The distance of 78 *li* can be covered by train in approximately one and a half hours and His Majesty ordered that this railway be completed within six months, but only four months were required. The cost was no more than 600,000 taels of silver."

The next project was the manufacture of the imperial "dragon train". Seizing an opportunity to enrich themselves while currying favour with the Empress Dowager and the throne, Sheng Xuanhuai and Yuan Shikai spent imperial funds recklessly. Quoting from *Collected Articles on the History of the Ming and Qing Dynasties*: "The coach built for Empress Dowager Cixi contains an iron bed complete with mattress, quilts and blankets. Unlike those in an ordinary coach, this bed has been specifically designed to suit the requirements of her opium-smoking habit. Placed crosswise in the car facing the window and hidden behind a curtain, the height of its legs have been shortened while its main section has been elevated. A bedside door leads into a closet containing a chamber pot filled with a mixture of sand and mercury into which the stool drops and disappears without leaving a trace. The chamber pot is covered with a large cloth cover so that outwardly it resembles an embroidered cushion. The walls of the coach are lined with silk and faced with yellow woollen fabric." It was believed that this type of chamber pot was the finest available at the time. Inside the coach, the floor is covered with brightly coloured carpets of foreign manufacture. The interior is also decorated with antiques, jade carvings, and famous works of Chinese calligraphy and painting. The same book continues, "Entering the coach, the first thing one sees is a glass screen. The door, in the southeast corner, opens into a big room in the centre of which stands a throne graced by dragon-patterned covers of shimmering yellow silk. The throne is surrounded by long tables and imported carpets are spread over the floor. There are smaller doors on either side of the dragon throne, the one on the left connected with a hallway that leads to the back door of the coach and the one on the right giving access to a smaller inner room."

Emperor Guangxu's coach was just as elaborate as the Empress Dowager's. As for the empress, imperial concubines and princes, they had to content themselves with second-class coaches, while the rear coach of the train was reserved for eunuchs.

When the construction of the train was completed, the chief eunuch Li Lianying came to inspect it. Satisfied, he praised his underlings for their "cleverness".

The train was tested by Sheng Xuanhuai and Yuan Shikai. "Seeing the antiques and scrolls decorating the coaches," the source mentioned above continues, "Yuan said, 'They are satisfactory for gracing the interior of the train, but they may tilt and fall when the train jolts. Who will be there to answer for that before His and Her Majesties?' 'Would Your Excellency please test the train when it is running at top speed?' asked Sheng. 'If the works of art move from their original position, we shall try to find a way of solving the problem.' The train was run back and forth between the Beijing west station and Dingxing in the southwest, a round trip covering a total distance of 200 *li* taking some two hours. Every object in the coaches remained precisely where they were supposed to be." Only after the completion of this test run was an auspicious departure time chosen for the Empress Dowager and the emperor's journey: the morning of the eighth day of the third month of the twenty-ninth year of the Guangxu reign.

Because Li Lianying did not approve of the ordinary method of boarding a train, "a makeshift gangplank covered with multi-coloured carpet was arranged enabling the Empress Dowager to be carried into the coach, thus saving her the trouble of stepping up the precarious iron steps at the coach entrance. All she needed to do was grasp its railing."

Accompanying the Empress Dowager on her trip to the Western Tombs were Emperor Guangxu, his empress and concubines, Prince Qing and a number of senior officials. Guangxu arrived at the railway station first, and was the first to kneel down to greet the Empress Dowager when she arrived. The train stopped en route whenever she felt like eating. "The emperor dined with the Empress Dowager, with his empress and concubines standing in attendance behind them. The dishes were brought into her coach through the southeast door and the left-overs were taken away through the northwest door. This procession continued like a running stream right up to the end of the meal. The emperor only took something to eat with his chopsticks when the Empress Dowager did so. She handed empty bowls to his empress and concubines, who then began eating cautiously, not knowing themselves how much food they had swallowed. Everybody would mechanically stop eating the moment the Empress Dowager's chopsticks stopped moving. . . . The emperor, empress and concubines always had to behave this way when eating in the presence of the Empress Dowager. It was quite a task for them. When she ordered a left-over dish to be given to an official as a gift, cries of

'Prince Qing thanks Her Majesty for her imperial favour', 'Yuan Shikai thanks Her Majesty for her imperial favour', 'Sheng Xuanhuai thanks Her Majesty for her imperial favour' would be heard echoing through the length of the train. The loud cries inside the coaches plus the kowtowing outside created quite a commotion."

According to *A Sequel to "Annals of the Qing Dynasty"*, two days after her trip to the Western Tombs Empress Dowager Cixi issued a decree saying, "All the prefectures and counties we passed through during our recent visit to the Western Tombs, namely, Wanping, Liangxiang, Zhuozhou, Xincheng, Laishui, Yixian, Fangshan, Qingyuan, Dingxing and Ansu should be granted the favour of paying only seven-tenths of their tax and tribute grain to the court for the current year." Such hypocrisy should come as no surprise to anyone familiar with the history of this period.

MISS CARL PAINTS
A PORTRAIT OF EMPRESS
DOWAGER CIXI

Liu Guilin

Historical records show that, at the turn of the century, an American woman named Katherine Augusta Carl painted a portrait of Empress Dowager Cixi. Though this cannot be considered a significant event, it does shed some light on the character of "Old Buddha", who virtually ruled the Qing Dynasty for nearly five decades.

Cixi often said, "As long as I am around, nobody is allowed to emulate foreigners." Whenever it suited her, however, she made exceptions to her own rule. For not only did she make use of various imported objects in the palace, she also had an American artist paint a portrait of her so that the whole world might be able "to admire her imperial appearance".

According to Chinese tradition, the descendants of a deceased person could have a portrait of the deceased painted for the purpose of offering sacrifices. The Qing Emperor Qianlong (reigned 1736-1796) ordered two

Western priests who served as court painters to paint "the divine appearance" of his dead mother. This is why, when Mrs. Edwin Hund Conger (wife of the American minister to the Qing court) visited Cixi and suggested that Miss Carl paint her portrait, Old Buddha (as the Empress Dowager Cixi was called by eunuchs) was at a loss what to say. She made up her mind, however, when she learned that the portrait would be sent to an exhibition in the American city of St. Louis. Though she hated to give up an opportunity to allow the American people to "admire" her appearance, Cixi did not think it appropriate to accept the proposal then and there. So she said that she could not "make an arbitrary decision" on the matter, which "should be first discussed with the court officials", adding, "I must abide by the principles set down by my ancestors and by Chinese custom." After Mrs. Conger's departure, Cixi became impatient and asked her chief eunuch, "Why should I have to sit for my portrait? Couldn't somebody else sit for it on my behalf?" "Should I wear the same dress and the same jewellery I wear every day?" "How long will it take to finish the painting?" and so on and so forth. A few days later, Prince Qing came and asked her to fix a date for Miss Carl to begin the painting. "I'll choose an auspicious day for it," Cixi said, "and let her know tomorrow." Then she leafed through an almanac. It was clear that she made the "arbitrary decision" herself without bothering to "abide by the rules of her ancestors or of Chinese custom".

According to the archives of the Qing Dynasty Board of Foreign Affairs, Prince Qing wrote to Minister

Conger that Mrs. Conger was to bring Miss Carl to the Summer Palace to paint Cixi's portrait.

Every year, Cixi spent her summers in the Summer Palace. Since she thought it would be too inconvenient for Miss Carl to commute between Beijing proper and her summer resort, she had the nearby Mansion of Prince Chun tidied up for her to stay in, and ordered a noble woman, Mme. Yugeng, and her two daughters (Rong Ling and Der Ling) to keep Miss Carl company and prevent her from coming into contact with any other people, especially Emperor Guangxu. On the night of the 14th day of the sixth month of the 29th year of the Guangxu reign (1903), Cixi, who was then nearly seventy, turned in earlier than usual in order to be "full of vigour" for the major event the next day.

Miss Carl arrived at the Summer Palace on the appointed day, accompanied by Mrs. Conger. The American artist, who had studied for years in France, specialized in figure painting. Elegant in appearance and well aware of how to behave in the presence of a Chinese woman ruler, she found herself in Cixi's good graces the moment they met. After a brief chat in her living quarters in the Hall of Joyful Longevity, Old Buddha went into her bed chamber and changed into a yellow robe embroidered with purple peonies draped with a light shawl decorated with pearls and the Chinese character "Longevity". Her headdress was festooned with jade butterflies and fresh flowers, and she wore jade bracelets on her wrists and long nailguards on her fingers. Outside, Miss Carl was waiting, pallet in hand.

Cixi emerged and settled herself on the throne, but before long she began to feel tired. The next morning, she sat only for ten minutes before suggesting that stand-ins sit on her behalf while Carl was painting her dress, promising to reappear when it came time to portray her face. Her understudies for this role were Princesses Rong Ling and Der Ling.

Work on the portrait progressed slowly. By the eighth month, Cixi had become tired of the whole affair and repeatedly asked Miss Carl when it would be completed. In the presence of Mrs. Conger, she praised the American artist for her efforts, but continually complained behind her back. "The painting is too vulgar," she said to Der Ling. "A Chinese painter can portray a person after observing him or her just once. But Miss Carl isn't capable of that, so she can't be considered a good painter." Unsure of whether the painting would ever be finished, Cixi even tried to back out, saying, "I'm tired of sitting on the throne for the painting." More ridiculously, she evaluated Carl's artistic ability by the way she had coloured pearls in white, light blue and pink. Old Buddha insisted that all pearls were white, and it never occurred to her that an artist would colour them according to the way they reflected the light.

It took nearly ten months for the portrait to be completed. One week before the finishing touches were added, Cixi discovered that one half of her face was darker than the other. Quite displeased, she demanded that this be "corrected", and the American artist complied under protest. The old woman was even surprised when the foreigner signed her name at the bottom of her work.

Despite her complaints and arbitrary criticism, Cixi

behaved rather politely to the artist. She gave her gifts on numerous occasions and publicly praised Miss Carl as being "a capable and skilled painter". That Cixi allowed this Carl to stay in her own Summer Palace was more than a friendly gesture. Two weeks after the start of the work on her portrait, Old Buddha ordered the Department of Imperial Court Affairs to present four baskets of fruit and two cooked dishes to Carl. Two months later, the chief eunuch Li Lianying sent to the Board of Foreign Affairs eight cooked dishes, four types of pastry and two sacks of polished rice to be delivered to the American painter. Four months after that, Miss Carl received four pots of flowers, two bricks of Pu'er Tea from Yunnan and four boxes of cakes through the same channel. On another occasion, eight boxes of pastry were sent to Carl. Four days after this, the head of the Board of Foreign Affairs visited the American legation in Beijing to relay Cixi's satisfaction with Carl's work and presented Miss Carl with a medal, eight bolts of fine dress material, 12 rolls of embroidered silk braids and a bank draft for 12,000 taels of silver, as remuneration for her creative efforts. One month after the completion of the portrait, Cixi gave her American friend a parcel of rare delicacies including bird's nests and snow mushrooms.

Over the course of one year, Miss Carl painted four portraits of Cixi. The Customs Commissioner, acting on an order from the Board of Foreign Affairs, sent one of them to St. Louis for exhibition. Later it was taken to Washington by Zhang Quan, Under-Secretary of the Board of Revenue, and presented to President Theodore Roosevelt on January 15, 1905 at a ceremony attended by Liang Cheng, the Qing ambassador to the United States, Peru, Cuba and Mexico. Both Liang and Roosevelt spoke on this occasion. The portrait was afterwards sent to the National Gallery in Washington.

THE GRAND COUNCIL SECRETARY STEALS GOLD SEAL OF HEAVENLY KING

Yang Naiji

Despite the strict security measures taken in the Forbidden City, there were frequent cases of theft involving palace orderlies, eunuchs and other attendants who resorted to larceny to increase their incomes. It was usually gold, silver, jewellery, or valuable household utensils that they would steal which, once smuggled out of the palace, they would either pawn or sell. Those who were eventually arrested by palace detectives were sentenced to either beheading, caning or exile.

The case of palace larceny described below is out of the ordinary for the following reasons: First, the thief was neither a palace orderly nor a eunuch, but the sanctimonious Salonga, a law enforcement official employed in the capacity of a senior secretary in the Board of Punishments, as well as a Manchu secretary of the Grand Council, a position popularly known as "Little Councillor". Second, the crime took place in the most heavily guarded section of the palace, the office of the

Grand Council on the west side of the Gate of Heavenly Purity, where no one — not even Grand Secretaries, court ministers or princes unless they were working in the Grand Council itself — was allowed to enter. Third, the stolen object was the precious captured 110-ounce gold seal of Hong Xiuquan, Heavenly King of the Taiping Heavenly Kingdom during the famous Taiping Revolution (1851-1864), a peasant movement finally suppressed by the Qing regime.

Historical records show that Salonga was the highest-ranking Qing official to have stolen anything from the palace, and that the stolen article was of inestimable political value.

This imperial seal of pure gold bore eight Chinese characters: "Gold Seal — Long Live the Taiping Heavenly Kingdom". Originally preserved in the official residence of the Heavenly King in Tianjing (now Nanjing), the capital of the Taiping kingdom, it was captured together with two jade imperial seals by the Qing troops when they occupied Tianjing in 1864, the third year of the Tongzhi reign (1862-1874). Not long afterwards, Zeng Guofan (1811-1872), then the Governor-General of Jiangsu, Jiangxi and Anhui Provinces, had the three treasures delivered to Beijing. They were examined by Emperor Tongzhi and Empress Dowagers Ci'an and Cixi before being turned over to the Grand Council for safekeeping.

The next year, the gold seal was reported missing. "It is harder to guard against a thief in the family than against an outsider," so runs a Chinese saying. On the 17th day of the eighth month of that year, "Little Councillor" Salonga helped himself to this much treasured trophy. As recorded in the archives of the De-

123

partment of Imperial Court Affairs, when Salonga arrived at the office of the Grand Council for work early that morning, he found the strong-box in the office of the Han secretaries open — apparently another official had removed something from it earlier that day for official purposes — and stealthily removed the seal of the Heavenly King. On the 24th he took the seal to the Wanshengchang Jewellery Shop near the Dongsi Market Arch where, at a cost of six silver dollars and with the help of shop assistants Wang Tai and Wang Quan, had it smelted into ten gold bars each weighing about 11 ounces. Burying eight of them in the ash-pit of his fireplace, he exchanged the other two for silver dollars at the Henghe Money Shop.

The records state that Salonga not only "had the heart of a jackal and the gall of a tiger, but also knew how to shift blame upon others and dispose stolen articles." It was customary practice when a case of larceny occurred in the palace that the first suspects to be interrogated were the orderlies and eunuchs, no one would ever suspect a secretary of the Grand Council, for the appointment of these officials went through a process of recommendation by the department in which they served, examination by the Grand Councillors themselves and the personal approval of the emperor. Secretaries of the Manchu nationality were chosen from among the junior or senior secretaries of the cabinet, metropolitan boards or the Department of Mongolia, Tibet and Xinjiang Affairs. Of the 32 "Little Councillors" appointed at the time, Salonga was one of the highest-ranking.

As stated above, the larceny took place in the office of the Grand Council secretaries of the Han nationality, men in charge of external liaison and thus responsible for the safekeeping of the gold seal turned in by Governor-General Zeng Guofan. Thus Salonga, who worked in another room reserved for the Manchu secretaries, could say easily that he was in no way involved with the missing seal. He could also argue that the treasure was stolen either before or after his arrival at the office that day. Furthermore, the seal had already been smelted down, and "A thief must be caught together with the stolen goods in order to bring a charge against him," as a Chinese saying goes. As expected, all the palace orderlies and cooks were detained and cross-examined on order of Prince Gong, then the highest-ranking member of the Grand Council and head of the Department of Imperial Court Affairs. No one pleaded guilty, however, so to crack the larceny case, palace detectives were sent beyond the walls of the Forbidden City to investigate.

The detectives soon learned that the Wanshengchang Jewellery Shop had recently smelted a gold seal for a customer. Wang Tai and Wang Quan made a complete confession, whereupon Salonga was arrested and charged with the crime. At first he refused to plead guilty, but changed his story when confronted with the confession of the two shop assistants. A house search uncovered the eight gold bars and some of the silver dollars. Salonga was cashiered from all his official posts and handed over to the Board of Punishments for "trial and punishment according to law".

In an imperial edict of the twelfth month of the same year, Salonga was sentenced to be hanged in the late autumn of the coming year. The palace detectives who solved the case were granted sinecures one grade above their respective posts.

The Salonga scandal brought disgrace to the Tongzhi reign which had just carried out "resurgence" of the quickly declining Qing empire. Small wonder that the government did not want the public to know too much about the case, and that both the punishment meted out to the criminal and the rewards given to the "meritorious" detectives were moderate. An interesting addition to the case came in the form of a memorial presented to the throne by an untactful supervising official named Zhang Guanjun, in which he stated, "Since imperial officials who break the law shall be punished more severely than commoners, Salonga's case ought to be reconsidered and his new sentence carried out immediately." Zhang had the courage to add the following, "Should Salonga, whose crime is so serious that even heaven and earth shall condemn him for it and neither the people nor the imperial officials can tolerate it, escape the death penalty, there will be no way to appease the whole nation, which unanimously demands his execution."

Zhang Guanjun's memorial reflected, to a degree, the public opinion of the time. Nevertheless, whether or not Salonga had influential friends intervene on his behalf, the imperial regime finally chose to "reduce a big problem to a small one", if only in its own interests. Hence the following remark by the throne on Zhang's memorial: "Salonga is undoubtedly a degenerate. But since imperial law has been enforced impartially in connection with his case, and since the Board of Punishments has dealt with his offence in compliance with the law, it is inappropriate to discuss whether the punishment is proper."

This statement is the height of absurdity. If the Qing Dynasty could have suppressed the popular movement of the Taiping Heavenly Kingdom by slaughtering multitudes of peasant rebels, including numerous captives, why should it hesitate to execute a man who was guilty of committing larceny right under the emperor's nose? Could this be termed "impartial enforcement of the law"? Even now, for lack of historical evidence, no one knows for certain if the despicable Grand Council secretary was ever hanged for his crime "in the late autumn of the coming year".

EUNUCHS BEATEN UP
AT THE MERIDIAN GATE

Liu Guilin

One morning in the autumn of 1881, Empress Dowager Cixi ordered the young eunuch Li Sanshun to deliver some gifts to her younger sister, the consort of Prince Chun whose son became Emperor Guangxu seven years ago. Li had two palace orderlies pack the things in two baskets, and then the three of them set out to leave the Forbidden City for Prince Chun's residence.

When they reached the Meridian Gate, they were stopped by two guards named Zhonghe and Changhe and the officer on duty who demanded from them documents authorizing them to remove things from the palace. Li Sanshun explained that all he had was a list of the gifts they were carrying, and that no authorization was needed when gifts were being delivered to princes or court ministers. But the duty officer and guards would not let them go. Li became very angry and walked towards the Gate of Flourishing Fortune to speak with the guards commander. But before he had taken more than a few paces he was called back and cuffed and kicked by two other guards named Yulin and Xiangfu, who dragged the eunuch to the Meridian Gate where he fell to the flagstone-paved walk. The pain of an injury he had sustained in the left side of his chest was so great that Li lost consciousness.

At this point another eunuch named Liu Yuxiang heard the hubbub and came to offer assistance. Seeing Li Sanshun lying unconscious on the pavement, he turned round and announced that he was going to report this to his superior. Zhonghe pulled the eunuch back by his queue so roughly that he pulled off a tuft of his hair and injured his left arm before he fell on the ground.

In his memorial to the throne, Yulin, the commander of the palace guards, described the cause of the incident as the eunuchs' defying the regulations and provoking a quarrel with the guards. Emperor Guangxu, however, learned the truth from other sources and decreed: "Although strict security measures are called for at the various gates of the Forbidden City, it is an outrage for a palace guard to beat up a gift-bearing eunuch without first making the proper inquiries. The Department of Imperial Court Affairs and the Board of Punishments are hereby instructed to put the palace guards involved in the incident on trial."

Accordingly, Encheng and four other ministers of the Department of Imperial Court Affairs; Wenyu and Pan Zuyin, who were in charge of the Board of Punishments; and a medical examiner, carried out an investigation, including a physical examination of the injured eunuchs. Li Sanshun and Liu Yuxiang's injuries were confirmed, and the four guards were interrogated. The officials concluded that beating up the eunuchs was indeed an outrage, and instructed their subordinates to investigate further whether the whole incident had arisen from personal grudges. Thus the palace guards were subjected to further interrogation during which they flatly denied any personal enmity against the eunuchs. Later, 16 officials from the Department of Imperial Court Affairs, the Board of Punishments and other related offices submitted a joint memorial to Emperor Guangxu, proposing flogging, wearing the cangue in public and whipping as punishment for the guards. His Majesty read the memorial but ordered a further inquiry.

In the course of the third interrogation which was coupled with torture, Yulin insisted that Li Sanshun's injury resulted from his falling on the flagstone pavement, and that he had neither cuffed nor kicked the young eunuch. Encheng and the other officials proposed the same basic punishments for the guards as detailed in their previous memorial. Still unsatisfied, the emperor demanded another round of interrogations. The following day, Empress Dowager Ci'an issued a decree of her own, requesting that Li Sanshun and the four palace guards be brought to the Department of Imperial Court Affairs.

In Li's presence, the four guards tried to defend themselves, finally confessing their offence under repeated torture. They disavowed any prejudice against the victims, however. In their joint memorial to the throne, Encheng and the other officials proposed the following penalties for the offenders:

Zhonghe — expulsion from the palace guards, one hundred strokes of the bamboo and exile to a place 1,500 km. from Beijing. Since he belonged to the imperial Gioro clan, a three-year period of detention and forty strokes of the bamboo were accepted in place of his exile.

Yulin — expulsion from the palace guards, one hundred strokes of the bamboo and exile to a point 1,000 km from Beijing. As an additional punishment, he was to wear the cangue in public for three months, submit to flogging and perform forced labour in Jilin for three years.

Xiangfu — expulsion from the palace guards, wear the cangue for three months, one hundred strokes of the bamboo and exile to a frontier region for three years of forced labour.

As Changhe did not take part in beating up the eunuchs, he was not punished.

Three days later, however, Emperor Guangxu, acting on instructions from Empress Dowager Ci'an, decreed heavier punishment for the offenders: "Yulin and Xiangfu are to be expelled from the palace guards and from the ranks of Bannermen; they are hereby banished to Heilongjiang to perform forced labour. No amnesty will be shown to them. Zhonghe is to be expelled from the palace guards and detained for five years. These punishments are in addition to the flogging and wearing of the cangue as previously stipulated."

Some weeks later, Chen Baochen (1852-?) whose task was to keep daily records of palace activities memorialized the throne, stating that the penalties for the palace guards were unreasonably severe. "Bannermen are only deprived of their status in the Eight Banners if they commit rape, larceny or swindling. Only the most vicious robbers and murderers should be denied imperial amnesty. As it is, manhandling resulting in bodily injuries is not a serious offence, and even serious lawlessness should not bar offenders from the benefits of amnesty. What is more, a five-year period of detention for members of the imperial Gioro clan is an extremely heavy penalty."

Within three days of the receipt of this memorial, the Empress Dowagers Ci'an and Cixi issued a joint instruction granting "extraordinary imperial favour" to Yulin and Xiangfu, who were allowed to retain their Banner membership, and to Zhonghe, whose detention was reduced to two years. Meanwhile, the eunuch Li Sanshun was given 30 strokes of the bamboo and the veteran eunuch Liu Yuxiang was fined a sum equalling six months' salary.

EUNUCH TROUBLE-MAKERS

Zhong Jin

Drawing on the lessons of the Ming Dynasty which suffered appallingly from the eunuchs' usurpation of power, the early Qing government repeatedly issued decrees forbidding their intervention in state administration. The Kangxi Emperor (reigned 1662-1722) even ordered that, for their crimes, court eunuchs should be punished more severely than others. Increasing corruption in the later years of the dynasty, however, emboldened these castrated men to behave more and more lawlessly. In the fourth year of his reign, Emperor Daoguang (reigned 1821-1850) felt it necessary to promulgate the following: "Except when on purchasing missions, no eunuchs are allowed to idle outside the palace walls. They are forbidden to go to theatres or wine shops. Those who break these rules shall be dealt with without delay." But during the Xianfeng reign (1851-1861), and particularly during the rule of Empress Dowager Cixi, when the chief eunuch Li Lianying wormed his way into her good graces, the situation worsened steadily. The eunuchs were seen swaggering about in every corner of Beijing, even in the neighbourhood of Dashala outside the Front Gate, where gangsters held sway. This, along with the weakness of the garrison troops and *yamen* personnel, none of whom dared to offend the neuters, was the reason why the eunuchs caused so much trouble — and even bloodshed — in the imperial capital.

UPROAR IN A THEATRE

At noon on the 18th day of the fourth month in 1896 the 22th year of the Guangxu reign, eunuchs Li Changcai of the Palace of Eternal Harmony, Zhang Shoushan of the Palace of Concentrated Beauty and Yan Baowei of the Palace of Aggregate Purity left the Forbidden City together to seek pleasure. They met another eunuch, Fan Lianyuan, not far from the Gate of Heavenly Peace. After some discussion, the four of them headed for the Qinghe Theatre in Dashala.

After entering the theatre, the eunuchs went upstairs, where they found three boxes with excellent views of the stage. As they got down, they were told by an attendant that those seats were already reserved. While the four argued back, the man who had booked the three boxes arrived and refused to let the eunuchs have their way. Li Changcai shouted abuses at him, and a nasty quarrel broke out. It was only after Hei Yong, proprietor of the theatre, managed to calm the eunuchs down and ushered them into his office that the uproar subsided. But that was not the end of it. The four demanded that the proprietor hold the man who had reserved the seats in his theatre until they came back to settle accounts with him.

Out in the street, Li Changcai, still fuming, suggested that they teach the man a lesson, and the other three agreed. Li, Yan and Zhang each obtained daggers, and Fan found a thick club. They also asked three of their kind — Wang Lianke, Li Laixi and Wu De'e — and a commoner named Bi Wenlu to help them. At about four o'clock the same afternoon, the eight of them entered the Qinghe Theatre to seek their revenge.

To avoid trouble, the man the eunuchs were after had already left, so they got hold of the proprietor Hei Yong, who had to beg them for mercy. The eight trouble-makers demonstrated their strength by smashing everything in Hei's office. A performance was going on in the theatre at this time, and when the audience heard the commotion, they all left. In the ensuing confusion, the proprietor also disappeared. The theatre attendants implored the smashers to stop by kowtowing to them, and then invited them to the nearby Tianquan Teahouse for a brief rest.

BLOODSHED IN THE TEAHOUSE

Once he escaped from the scene of the disturbance, Hei Yong reported to the police, and an officer named Zhao Yunqi was dispatched to the Qinghe Theatre along with twenty soldiers to restore peace.

When Zhao learned that the eunuchs were in the Tianquan Teahouse, he led his men there, and charged into the building with four of them leaving the rest waiting outside.

The eunuchs' resistance caused Zhao to have his

135

soldiers arrest them. An armed struggle ensued, during which Li Changcai cracked open the skull of one of the soldiers with his dagger, while another eunuch, Fan Lianyuan, struck the victim where it hurt most. The soldier fell to the ground, unconscious. When another of Zhao's men was wounded by Yan Baowei, Fan repeated what he had done to the other soldier.

With two of his men seriously wounded, Zhao Yunqi swooped down upon the eunuchs, first engaging Zhang Shoushan, who was madly wielding his dagger in all directions. Zhao received cuts on his left forehead and his right shoulder, cheek and nose. He tried to retaliate by jerking Zhang's long queue. Struggling to free himself, the desperate eunuch thrust his weapon into the left side of Zhao's chest. Just as Zhao was about to escape, Zhang stabbed him again in the chest, and Zhao fell down bleeding profusely.

The bloody fight which made a shambles of the teahouse attracted many passers-by. They were indignant at the brutalities of the eunuchs and surrounded them preventing them from making their escape. The four eunuchs and Bi Wenlu were arrested by the soldiers. Only Li Laixi, Wang Lianke and Wu De'e managed to flee back to the Forbidden City.

A VETERAN EUNUCH DISRUPTS THE INQUEST

The following day, Zhao Yunqi died of multiple wounds. The news aroused the Beijing residents' intense hatred of the lawless eunuchs, and so many of them appeared at the morgue when the eunuch bloodletters were escorted there for the inquest that traffic was blocked. Suddenly, a man jumped out of the crowds, shouting in a feminine voice, and obstructed the soldiers' procession. When a soldier tried to drive him away, the intruder swore and beat him. He was then arrested.

The intruder was Chen Heyu, a veteran eunuch who worked in the Palace of Vigorous Old Age. He had just returned from home leave, and noticing several of his colleagues being escorted by soldiers, thought this was a disgrace to his kind. But when he rose to the occasion, he never expected that he would be arrested.

Inquest confirmed that Zhao Yunqi's death was due to severe dagger wounds. Li Changcai and the other eunuchs had to accept this fact and sign the coroner's report.

According to Qing law, eunuchs guilty of major criminal offences were handed over to the Board of Punishments for trial. This became the fate of Li Changcai and the other criminals.

EMPEROR GUANGXU'S EDICT

Following detailed investigation, Guinian, an official in the imperial Censorate, wrote a memorial to Emperor Guangxu, urging that the eunuchs involved be punished according to law for creating a public disturbance and for committing homicide. To support his position, he cited in an appendix several precedents of Emperors Kangxi and Daoguang.

Emperor Guangxu, who detested the corrupt politics

of the time and was planning a large-scale reform of the imperial government, flew into a rage when he read Guinian's memorial. On the 22nd day of the fourth month of the year, he issued the following decree: "Severe penalties must be meted out to the palace eunuchs who defied the public security soldiers and killed their leader Zhao Yunqi. The five eunuchs, namely, Li Changcai, Zhang Shoushan, Yan Baowei, Fan Lianyuan and Chen Heyu, and the commoner Bi Wenlu should be tried and punished according to law by the Board of Punishments. As for those criminals still at large, they should be prosecuted without fail." His Majesty also emphasized the necessity of abiding by edicts issued by former emperors regarding the punishment of law-breaking eunuchs.

The trial of the criminals was presided over by Xue Yunsheng, the Han-nationality Minister of Punishments. He first had the Department of Imperial Court Affairs hand over for trial Li Laixi and the two other eunuchs at large. The department, however, replied, "The eunuchs have escaped. No deadline can be set for their arrest." Although this was clearly an act of shielding the three eunuchs, Xue could do nothing about it because the Forbidden City itself was involved.

In the trial, the Board of Punishments enlisted the co-operation of the Grand Court of Appeals and the Censorate. On 24th of the fourth month the three imperial departments submitted a joint memorial to the throne, proposing that Li Changcai and Zhang Shoushan be "summarily beheaded", that Fan Lianyuan and Yan Baowei be "hanged in late autumn", and that Bi Wenlu and Chen Heyu be "exiled to the frontier regions

2,000 km. from the imperial capital and imprisoned there for ten years".

THE CHIEF EUNUCH'S INTERCESSION

As their joint memorial had been drafted in compliance with Emperor Guangxu's edict, the three imperial departments thought there would be no difficulty in obtaining His Majesty's approval, and had a makeshift shed put up at the execution ground to carry out the stipulated punishments. The view brought to the spot huge crowds who were eager to see the end of the much hated eunuchs.

It was a rule in those days that criminals sentenced to death were executed at noon. The hour was approaching, yet there was no sign of the guilty eunuchs. Knowing for sure that something had gone wrong, the officials of the Board of Punishments took the expedient of executing a criminal named Zhao who had been condemned to death for engaging in an armed gang fight. This fraud, which at first baffled the public, eventually became an object of ridicule.

The true perpetration of this deception was Li Lianying, the chief palace eunuch and favourite of Empress Dowager Cixi. Considering the punishment of his men a discredit to his own prestige, Li sought out the good offices of his influential friends while interceding with the Empress Dowager on behalf of his criminal underlings. Emperor Guangxu, who found it difficult to go against any of Cixi's wishes, finally shelved the joint memorial from the three imperial departments on the grounds that it needed first to be submitted to Her Majesty.

PROTEST AND CONSEQUENCES

As a matter of fact, it required almost no effort for Cixi to alter the punishment of a eunuch. In this specific case, however, she needed a bit more tact than usual because the joint memorial to the throne was based on related decrees of former emperors. To avoid criticism for overstepping "ancestral rules", she decided that the convicted eunuchs should be dealt with as "guilty of unpremeditated manslaughter" which would make them liable to much lighter penalties.

This intervention from above landed Xue Yunsheng, the Minister of Punishments, in an embarrassing position. He resented Cixi's arbitrariness as much as the other officials. Meanwhile, the all-powerful eunuch asked several high-ranking officials to use any tactics they could to make Xue more flexible and realistic. The just-minded minister, however, remained firm in his stand. He drafted another memorial to the throne refuting the notion of "unpremeditated manslaughter" and regretting that "the earlier imperial edict was ignored". Reaffirming that "laws are enacted for the purpose of punishing evil-doers", he requested Emperor Guangxu to pass the joint proposals of the three imperial departments. "Should there be any intention to apply unlawful benevolence in this case," he said, "your subject chooses to refrain from making any other proposals."

This strongly worded and yet convincing petition put Empress Dowager Cixi in a dilemma, and she finally approved the death sentence for Zhang Shoushan, who had killed Zhao Yunqi with his own hands. Li Chang-cai received a new sentenced, "imprisonment pending beheading in late autumn", which, when the time of execution drew near, was changed to "beheading with reprieve". The other eunuch offenders only received sentences of exile.

But this show was not over yet. Both the Empress Dowager and her prime flunkey Li Lianying, who saw Xue Yunsheng as a thorn in their flesh, schemed to retaliate. First they had the Censorate impeach Xue for "embezzlement", an accusation which was turned down by the Board of Civil Office. Then they had him demoted by three grades and transferred out of the Board of Punishments on the pretext of his "never having dissociated himself" from a nephew who committed a criminal offence in the port city of Tianjin. Even Xue's son, a cabinet lecturer on the Confucian classics, was implicated and "fined nine months' salary". Xue Yunsheng retired due to "poor health" and moved his family to his native village in Chang'an, Shaanxi Province.

THE DEATH OF EMPEROR TONGZHI

Xu Yipu

When the young Emperor Tongzhi died in January 1875, it was less than two years after he had become the real sovereign and "freed" himself from the regency of his mother, Empress Dowager Cixi. Historians disagree on whether Tongzhi's death was due to smallpox, syphilis or scabies. This problem has been solved, however, with the recent discovery of a Qing document entitled "Records of Medical Prescriptions for Their Imperial Majesties", which provides precise data on the pulse and physiopathological conditions of the ailing emperor. Included in this corpus of materials are the texts of 160 prescriptions written by imperial physicians Li Deli and Zhuang Shouhe during the 37 days of Tongzhi's illness. In addition, the Chief Eunuch's Office made copies of the daily records of Tongzhi's pulse condition and medicine prescribed. These documents show beyond doubt that the eighth emperor of the Qing Dynasty died of smallpox, and no other causes.

I

When Tongzhi fell ill one afternoon approximately five weeks before his death, imperial physicians Li Deli and Zhuang Shouhe came immediately to examine His Majesty. Their diagnosis, in the language of traditional Chinese medicine, was: "Floating and thin pulse. Febrile disease, with heat blocked within. Deficiency of vital essence. Resultant fever, dizziness, chest stuffiness, restlessness, bodily soreness, laziness in limbs, partly hidden skin eruptions, laboured breathing, and lingering headache." The physicians prescribed twelve traditional medicines, including dried rhizome of reh-mannia, *fructus arctii* and reed root to reduce the heat and replenish the vital energy. The emperor took a dose that day. By the following morning, his skin eruptions became more noticeable and a number of pock marks appeared.

Due to too much internal heat, however, the pustules were particularly dense on Tongzhi's face and neck and turned dark purplish. He complained of pain in the throat and dryness in the mouth; he vomited and trembled all over. He was also constipated, and his urine became brownish in colour. The physicians diagnosed: "Stagnation of vital energy and blood due to extreme heat. Condition serious." They waited on him day and night. Two days later, his condition worsened. Apart from the previous clinical manifestations, Tongzhi began to complain of pain in the loins and pressure in the chest. His constipation continued for a fourth day. The diagnosis: "Morbid heat affecting the lungs and stomach. Deficiency of nurturing bodily fluid. Condition highly serious."

Five days later, the emperor was attacked by "wind and cold". He coughed, had a stuffy nose, and suffered from insomnia. His complications and the smallpox germs began to spread through his whole body. During the ensuing ten days, symptoms of dropsy appeared, and he began to breathe heavily. A deficiency of vital energy and blood, in particular, caused "drying up of the smallpox", and "bleeding of the scars when scratched".

On the morning of the 16th day of the 11th month, the following symptoms were detected: Weakening of the vital function of the kidney, morbid dampness in the bodily channels, and convulsions and stiffening in the legs. "Smallpox germs in the bodily channels" indicated that the disease was progressing beyond cure. Involuntary seminal discharge and passing of blood in the urine followed. The physicians prescribed medicine in an attempt to invigorate the function of the kidney and to detoxify his internal organs, but to no avail: By this point the complications were too numerous and the patient had become too weak.

II

Between the 19th and the 30th of the 11th month, Tongzhi suffered the worst from his illness. Internal infection combined with multiple carbuncles, mostly on his loins, caused him unbearable pain. Noxious breath and scanty urine were among the other new symptoms which appeared at this time.

The imperial physicians became extremely worried and wrote in Tongzhi's medical record: "It is hoped that the carbuncles will not penetrate the flesh to the bone." That is to say, were the carbuncular ulcers to grow much deeper, Tongzhi would have little chance to survive. But this was exactly what happened on the 25th when the affected areas began to spread, yielding a huge quantity of pus. The physicians washed his body with medicated solutions and applied hot compresses. The traditional Chinese medicines prescribed included monkshood, rhizome of Chinese atractylodes, pangolin scales and tendril-leaved frillary bulbs. But the physicians' efforts were in vain, for three days later the emperor ran a higher fever and sank into a coma.

On the 29th the physicians made the following entry in Tongzhi's medical file: "Vital energy failing to repress morbid factors. Condition deteriorating further. Imperial physicians unable to decide whether to apply warming and invigorating treatment or to prescribe anti-heat medicine." On the 30th, the patient became more sensitive to pain, a symptom which was interpreted as "the final glow of the setting sun" — a momentary recovery just before death.

Having survived through the last month of the year, Tongzhi was attacked by a fatal disease, stomatonecrosis. Despair and sorrow permeated the imperial palace as death descended on the body of the "Son of Heaven". And on the fifth day of the new year, he drew his last tormented breath.

III

Tongzhi's case history was recorded in some detail in *The Diaries of Weng Tonghe*. Weng Tonghe (1830-1904) came first in a highest imperial examination in Xianfeng reign and was a high official during Tong-zhi's reign and later became tutor of the succeeding Emperor Guangxu. What Weng Tonghe wrote generally agrees with the medical records quoted in the previous paragraphs. On his sickbed, Tongzhi summoned to his presence Prince Gong, Weng Tonghe and a number of other court officials. Weng wrote in his diary: "We approached His Majesty, who was lying on bed, his face turned towards us. His complexion was smooth and lustrous, his eyes half closed. His face was covered with dense smallpox eruptions." The next day, Weng and several senior Grand Councillors who came to see the emperor noticed that Tongzhi's head and face were covered with pus-filled eruptions. He even lifted an arm for them to see the smallpox more clearly.

Weng gave no hint at all that Tongzhi suffered from syphilis or any other disease which should have been kept a secret. Therefore, the allegation is unfounded that he died of venereal disease contracted as a result of frequent visits to the "willow lanes" of the city, on which occasions he disguised himself as a commoner.

AN INTRUDER
IN THE IMPERIAL PALACE

Liu Guilin

In dynastic times, the imperial palace was off limits to the common people. But in the archives of the Department of Imperial Court Affairs and the Board of Punishments of the Qing Dynasty, an incident is recorded of a lunatic stealing into the Hall of Supreme Harmony where the emperor attended to affairs of state. He even performed a dance there, little aware that a noose was hovering over his head.

The event took place in the summer of 1905, in the final years of the Guangxu reign. One late summer day that year, the gate guards of the imperial palace were making their rounds of the four major entrances to the palace. At first they found nothing abnormal. But as they patrolled slowly from the Hall of Preserved Harmony to the Hall of Central Harmony and then to the Hall of Supreme Harmony they suddenly noticed a broken window frame in the emperor's throne hall. Halting to examine the scene, they heard movements inside, and immediately reported this to the officer on duty and the key keeper, who sought further instructions from Douqin, the minister in charge of the strategic Gate of Flourishing Fortune. Douqin lost no time in bringing the matter before the minister in charge of imperial palace affairs. Together with the officers on duty responsible for the security of the three major halls, they proceeded to the Hall of Supreme Harmony, and opening the door, found a man dancing on the floor. He was immediately arrested and subjected to a body search which yielded the following: a short sheathed dagger, a small knife, and a cloth bundle containing two boxes of matches, nine copper coins, a piece of paper currency and 760 copper cash. A smaller bundle inside the larger one was found to contain a piece of carved jade, a grey sash, a linen jacket, a short tobacco pipe, a fan, a snuff bottle, a purple pebble and a floral-patterned towel.

For an armed outsider to intrude into the Forbidden City was no trivial matter. When Douqin and the others had him interrogated, they learned that his name was Jia Wanhai, that he was 29 years old, and that he lived in Daxing County in the outskirts of Beijing. Further interrogation, however, revealed that he was incapable of speaking coherently, and thus the officials suspected he was a lunatic. Since it was difficult to continue the cross-examination, the minister in charge of the Gate of Flourishing Fortune reported the case to Empress Dowager Cixi and Emperor Guangxu the next day, suggesting that Jia Wanhai be handed over to the Board of Punishments together with the dagger and other objects found on him. An imperial decree came down the same day, approving the delivery of the uninvited guest to the Board of Punishments for trial.

During the ensuing trial, Jia looked as disoriented as before and his confession was confused and inconsistent. He was examined by a physician who diagnosed "mental disturbance due to excess heat in the liver and phlegmatic fire". The judge, therefore, ordered medical treatment for the demented intruder. When he was re-tried one month later, however, his condition had not improved and he was unable to say anything credible. But since he had intruded into the imperial palace and been arrested by the palace guards, and, since his case had been handed down by the Board of Punishments, it had to be dealt with without delay. According to Qing Dynasty law, trespassing into the Forbidden City with any object that could cause physical harm was punishable by hanging. With the approval of the throne, Jia Wanhai was hanged after a third trial.

Who, then, was responsible for an incident which was clearly due to negligence of duty? Due to Jia's insanity, it was impossible to learn when, where and how he had entered the imperial palace. And more specifically, how he found his way into the Hall of Supreme Harmony, of all places. The facts were that a lunatic had succeeded in breaking into the palace carrying a dagger, despite the successive lines of guards, and he had danced madly in the throne hall. Was Jia Wanhai really a lunatic? The incident remains an enigma.

A MAD MONK TRIES TO CRASH
THE PALACE GATE

One day in the winter of 1763, during the Qianlong reign, a monk by the name of Hongyu was seen staggering towards the Western Flowery Gate of the imperial palace, muttering to himself. The gate was closed at the time, with only a couple of guards standing before it. The monk demanded entry, which was, of course, refused. He insisted, however, talking wildly in the meantime. He was arrested and escorted to the officer on duty for interrogation. Subjected to torture, the monk spoke like an insane person, rendering the cross-examination useless. A physician from the Board of Punishments diagnosed that the monk was incapable of coherent speech, that his eyes were fixed in their sockets and that his jaw was abnormally rigid, all symptoms of mental derangement. The case was then referred to Brigadier Aligun who, acting on an imperial decree, managed to find the mad monk's master, a man named Benguang.

Through this old monk, the Board of Punishments learned that Hongyu was 29 years old and came from Changping Prefecture in the suburbs of Beijing. He became Benguang's disciple at the age of five, when the latter was abbot of a Buddhist temple in Hongyu's village. In 1761, the old man put Hongyu in charge of a small temple in a neighbouring village, but three years later Hongyu became mentally deranged for no discernible reason. His master was forced to take personal care of him, for Hongyu would occasionally climb onto a wall or onto the roof of a house and bother the neighbours, or open the door of his courtyard muttering that he was going to greet some arriving deities. Benguang hired a physician to treat his disciple, who responded well after taking several doses of traditional medicine. Pleased with Hongyu's recovery, the veteran monk relaxed his control and allowed Hongyu to roam freely about. One day in the winter of 1763, Hongyu attended a village fair and had a sudden relapse of his illness.

Considering the circumstances, the Board of Punishments had Hongyu escorted back to his village and placed in the custody of the local officials for the remainder of his life. As for Benguang, he was given 80 strokes of the bamboo.

THE TRUE CAUSE OF EMPEROR GUANGXU'S "SUDDEN DEATH"

Zhu Jinfu

On the 21st day of the tenth month in the 34th year of Guangxu's reign, the Qing throne became vacant once more. For the 38-year-old Guangxu (reigned 1875-1908) died in the Hall Preserving Vitality on Ocean Terrace Island in present-day Zhongnanhai Lake, where he had long been under house arrest by order of his aunt, Empress Dowager Cixi. He died in this isolated spot, nursing deep regrets over the failure of his Hundred-Day Reform of 1898 which was suppressed by Cixi, the Old Buddha. It so happened that, less than 24 hours after his death, the Old Buddha too departed from this world, ending her half-century grip on the reins of China's last feudal dynasty. This unusual coincidence quickly became the talk of the Middle Kingdom and the rest of the world as well. Many stories have been told about it, and many more about the death of Guangxu if only because of his bitter experience at the hands of the Old Buddha. Many people believe that he was poisoned. If so then, by whom? And how? The versions vary.

Some say that Empress Dowager Cixi, well aware of her own approaching end but reluctant to allow her rival Guangxu to regain power after her departure to join her ancestors, ordered a trusted follower to take his life. Others maintain that Cixi's chief eunuch Li Lianying, who was more than a mere flunkey of hers in persecuting Guangxu and who now dreaded the thought of persuing his career without the Empress Dowager, murdered him before her own last exit from the Qing court. Representatives of this school include John O. Bland and Edmund T. Backhouse, co-authors of *China Under the Empress Dowager* as well as the Qing Princess Der Ling. Still others judged that Guangxu died of poisoning by the perfidious hand of Yuan Shikai (1859-1916), who had betrayed the progressive emperor at a critical moment in the 1898 reform and who feared that he would have to pay for this treachery with his life once the Empress Dowager was gone. Most of the defenders of this version were court eunuchs, and the classic account appears in the autobiography of the last Qing monarch Puyi, in his book *From Emperor to Citizen*. One of the doctors who tried to save Guangxu's life three days before his death was named Qu Guiting. In an article on the subject, Qu wrote that the sovereign's condition deteriorated rapidly that day, and that he tossed wildly on his sickbed with stomach pain. Qu concluded that Guangxu died of poisoning, although he did not venture to guess who was behind the conspiracy.

These varied views add a distinct touch of mystery to the death of the second to last emperor of China.

Because Guangxu died within the palace grounds, no outsiders could provide any useful clues to the solution of this question. But now that it is possible to examine the thick file dealing with this case history preserved in the Palace Museum — including Guangxu's own oral and written description of his illness and the prescriptions written out for him by the imperial physicians — we are in a much better position to draw our own conclusions.

I

There is now little doubt that Guangxu's death at 38 was related to protracted physical weakness resulting from a lack of proper care and the numerous illnesses from which he suffered during his childhood. One year before his death, the emperor wrote, "I've been troubled by nocturnal emissions for almost two decades. It has occurred more than a dozen times a month during the last few years . . . especially in winter. . . . My legs and knees are always cold. . . . For nearly a decade, I have suffered frequently from buzzing in the ears . . . I am often sore in the loins, legs, back and shoulders." From diaries Guangxu wrote between the age of 14 and 16 we know that he frequently complained of pain in the spleen and stomach.

Apart from any congenital factors, Guangxu's poor physique was a result of the environment he lived in as a child. As the son of Empress Dowager Cixi's younger sister, who was the wife of Emperor Xianfeng's brother Prince Chun, Guangxu was placed on the throne by the Old Buddha after the death of Emperor Tongzhi, her own issueless son. Since Guangxu was only four years old at the time, Cixi became regent for the second time despite protests by many court officials. The new monarch's mother died shortly after his enthronement, and the power-thirsty Cixi made the child sovereign in order to retain imperial authority in her own hands, continuing to run state affairs "from behind a screen". Far from taking good care of the boy emperor, she often berated him and compelled him to learn all the complicated and annoying court etiquette. Living inside the Forbidden City under the watchful eyes of the Empress Dowager, Guangxu was deprived of the joys of a normal childhood. And there was no one to take care of his food, clothing and other daily needs. To quote *A Diary of Court Life*, written by Kou Liancai, one of Guangxu's favourite eunuchs, "All children can receive the benefits of parental love, and also the care of their parents with respect to food, clothing and daily activities. Even an orphan will have relatives or friends to provide for his needs. The only exception I know is His Majesty, whom no one dares to love at all. . . . Although the Son of Heaven, he is less happy than an orphan. A lack of proper care when he was a child has made him susceptible to disease." And as it is written in the *True Story of Emperor Guangxu's Life*, "The late Emperor Guangxu remained on the throne for a good number of years. . . . But he had no motherly love, no brotherly love, no love from a consort. He had no court ministers to keep him company in his leisure hour. Even a commoner lives a happier life than His Majesty, despite the fact that he stands above everyone else in terms of status."

II

It is apparent from Guangxu's medical history that his health improved somewhat between the age of 19 and 28, and that he took less medicine in that period than in previous years. Beginning from the age at 35, however, his physical condition took an abrupt downward turn. A number of complicated symptoms appeared. For instance, the physicians' diagnosis one day in 1899 was: "Deep and taut pulse alternating with slippery and thin pulse. Greyish-yellow complexion. Poor appetite. General fatigue. Lower half of torso damp and cold. Constipation. Frequent and sometimes difficult urination. Symptoms caused by deficiency of vital essence of the liver and spleen, defective function of the heart and presence of asthenic fire." These symptoms proved hard to eliminate because of their protracted character. Consequently, a physicians' report of one year later mentions that the illness had passed into Guangxu's "five viscera (heart, liver, spleen, lungs and kidneys)" and that there was a "deficiency of both vital energy and blood", symptoms indicative of a deterioration in his health. In modern medical terms, Guangxu was suffering from serious neurosis, arthritis (or bone tuberculosis) and haemopathy. Traditional Chinese medicine gives this condition the blanket term "chronic consumption".

What explains this sudden turn for the worse? Besides *causa morbi* dating back to the emperor's childhood, there was the psychological factor of his unhappy political career. After coming of age and marrying in 1889, although he took over from Cixi (whose regency was over according to "ancestral law"), Guangxu was ruler of China in name only. For the Empress Dowager, now 53 years old with over 26 years as the real sovereign of the Qing empire, was not resigned to a life of retirement in the Summer Palace. She tried to make Guangxu defer to her in all important court affairs and, at the same time, planted eunuch-spies in the Forbidden City to keep a watch on him. But now that he was able to judge things on his own, the emperor refused to play puppet any longer. Politically, he had been influenced by his Han tutor and a number of officials with progressive leanings. Soon after assuming the reins of government, he endeavoured to institute political reforms which met with desperate opposition from the Empress Dowager Cixi and her mandarin followers, for they saw in this a formidable menace to their vested interests. Hence the intense struggle between "the Dowager's Faction" and "the Emperor's Faction". In September 1898, the reform was stifled by the diehards represented by Cixi, who had the six chief reformists beheaded and the emperor himself placed under house arrest. She resumed her tutelage and did all she could to make the emperor's life miserable. As a result Guangxu suffered a nervous breakdown and a serious relapse of his illness, from which he was never to recover.

Although Cixi played a deleterious role in Guangxu's illness, his medical records do not suggest that the real cause of his death was murder. The fact is that after the failure of his political reform and the subsequent attack of his old illness, his health did not improve. By the spring of 1908, Guangxu was so grievously ill that murder was no longer necessary.

In April 1908, imperial physician Cao Yuanheng

wrote in Guangxu's case history that the emperor's deficiency of the vital essence of the liver, kidney and spleen and general debility were no longer responsive to either warming or cooling medicines. Two months later, another physician, Chen Bingjun, contributed the following: "Prolonged medicinal care has failed to produce any positive effect." By October, malfunctioning of all the emperor's internal organs was detected.

Guangxu was both increasingly worried about his condition and critical of his physicians. In July 1908, he made an entry in his medical records in which he criticized them for "aggravating my illness by constantly changing my prescriptions". In September, he wrote, "No medicines have been efficacious in curing my drawn-out illness. What's worse, one complication has followed another, and all have come to stay." Ten days later, he chided his physicians for "having failed to prescribe the proper medicine for my illness". About three weeks after that, he complained, "Each time they take my pulse,* they finish in a few moments. How can they possibly get to the bottom of my illness in this way? How can these reputedly expert physicians be so careless and incompetent?"

The seriousness of the monarch's illness at this time is referred to in the book *Notes on the Medical Treatment of Emperor Guangxu* by Du Zhongjun, a physician specially summoned to the imperial palace in the fall of 1908. After his first examination, Du confided his thoughts in a letter to Lu Runxiang (1841-1915),

---

* In traditional Chinese medicine, taking the pulse is the principal means of diagnosis, and may take as long as 15 minutes.

Minister of Civil Office, "I came to Beijing with the hope of doing my share in helping cure the emperor, and in this way better my own reputation. But now I see my efforts have been fruitless. Instead of striving to render any meritorious service, I will content myself with making no blunders."

A clear picture of how Guangxu died can be obtained by studying the medical records of the final few days of his life. His illness entered a critical stage around November 10, 1908. The previous day, there were symptoms of inflammation in the lungs and cardiac arrest. Three physicians, including Du Zhongjun, were called in the next day. They concluded that the end was near when they discovered a heat symptom-complex in the upper organs of the body and a cold symptom-complex in the lower organs, coupled with a serious deficiency of vital energy. As Du said to a Grand Councillor after leaving Guangxu's sickroom, "His Majesty has at most four days to live."

On the 12th, Guangxu's condition was described as follows: "Functional failure in the central portion of the body cavity with clogging of the channels there. Curative essence unable to overcome lingering morbid essence." From this point on, they only went through the motions of giving treatment. On the 13th, "the whites of his eyes were visible" and the corners of his lips were quivering, symptoms of the failure of the central nervous system. In the early hours of the next day, "His Majesty's pulse beat became extremely weak and nearly ceased. His limbs grew cold and his remaining vital energy began to sink. . . . He lost consciousness." By noontime, "The positive *yang* energy within His Majesty's body has been dissipated while the negative

159

yin energy has gained the upper hand." He drew his last breath by nightfall the same day.

Guangxu's medical records state that he died of several chronic consumptive diseases, including pulmonary tuberculosis, liver and heart disease and rheumatosis. The more immediate cause of his death was heart and lung failure combined with acute infection. Guangxu's symptoms worsened progressively, and there were no extraordinary symptoms suggesting poisoning or injuries to his person by others. All evidence points to the conclusion that his was a normal — not sudden — death.

APPENDIX:

Emperors of the Ming (1368-1644) and the Qing (1644-1911) Dynasties

Emperor Hongwu:

Zhu Yuanzhang (1368-1398). Placed in power by revolts of his fellow peasants in the south, toppled the Yuan Dynasty founded by Kublai Khan in Dadu (now Beijing). Established the Ming Dynasty and settled in Nanjing as his capital. As symbols of imperial authority, the Dadu Yuan palaces were dismantled by Emperor Hongwu. His tomb is in Nanjing.

Emperor Jianwen:

Zhu Yunwen (1399-1402). Grandson of Emperor Hongwu. Failed in strengthening the central imperial power in paring the princedoms, he was overthrown by his uncle, the fourth son of Emperor Hongwu, who made an expedition to Nanjing from his princedom capital Beiping (now Beijing). Emperor Jianwen disappeared.

Emperor Yongle:

Zhu Di (1403-1424). Moved the capital from Nanjing to Beiping and changed its name from Beiping to Beijing. Beijing's main architecture was built from 1405 to 1420. In Nanjing, a nominal government was also preserved. See p.7.

Emperor Hongxi:
　　Zhu Gaozhi (1425).

Emperor Xuande:
　　Zhu Zhanji (1426-1435).

Emperor Yingzong:
　　Zhu Qizhen (Zhengtong, 1436-1449). Usually called by his posthumous title "Emperor Yingzong", as the only emperor in both dynasties who had two reigning periods, i.e., the Zhengtong and Tianshun. See p. 14.

Emperor Jingtai:
　　Zhu Qiyu (1450-1456). Ascended to the throne as regent and soon became emperor when Emperor Yingzong was taken captive by the Mongolian Ye-xian tribe. Yingzong was sent back to Beijing the next year after his capture but was refused restoration to the throne. Emperor Jingtai was murdered by Yingzong after the South Palace Coup and was the only emperor not buried in the Ming Tombs. See p. 14.

Emperor Yingzong:
　　Zhu Qizhen (Tianshun 1457-1464). See p. 14.

Emperor Chenghua:
　　Zhu Jiansheng (1465-1487). See p. 14.

Emperor Hongzhi:
　　Zhu Youcheng (1488-1505). See p. 19.

Emperor Zhengde:
　　Zhu Houzhao (1506-1521). Led into a life of debauchery, he died without leaving an heir. Succeeded by his uncle's son.

Emperor Jiajing:

Zhu Houcong (1522-1566). Succeeded his cousin to the throne. As his father was not an emperor; His main objective, after his enthronement, was to confer on his father the posthumous title of emperor. Many upright officials who objected his doing so suffered death or torture, a way the Ming emperors chose to punish their ministers. He abandoned himself to Daoism and making elixir pills. He had for a score of years been absent from state affairs and not seen his ministers. See p. 29.

Emperor Longqing:

Zhu Zaihou (1567-1572).

Emperor Wanli:

Zhu Yijun (1573-1620). His mausoleum in the Ming Tombs is now open to the public. See p. 34.

Emperor Taichang:

Zhu Changluo (1620). Twenty-nine days after his enthronement, he died. See p. 35.

Emperor Tianqi:

Zhu Youjiao (1621-1627). See p. 39.

Emperor Chongzhen:

Zhu Youjian (1628-1644). Committed suicide by hanging under a locust tree in the back palace (now Jingshan Park) when the peasant army entered Beijing. Taking advantage of the chaotic situation, the Qing Dynasty superceded the Ming. See p. 52.

Emperor Shunzhi:

Aisin Gioro Fulin (1644-1661). See p. 55.

Emperor Kangxi:

Aisin Gioro Xuanye (1662-1722). Strengthened unification of the multi-national country and attached great importance to agricultural production. From his reign China's population began to grow enormously. See p. 55.

Emperor Yongzheng:

Aisin Gioro Yinzhen (1723-1735). Portrayed in chivalrous novels as one of high-handed policy.

Emperor Qianlong:

Aisin Gioro Hongli (1736-1795). Boasted of his reign as the most prosperous and styled himself as the "Ten-Perfect". See pp. 60, 64.

Emperor Jiaqing:

Aisin Gioro Yongyan (1796-1820). Peasant revolts burst out one after another. His reign witnessed the beginning of the decline of the dynasty. See pp. 68, 76, 86.

Emperor Daoguang:

Aisin Gioro Minning (1821-1850). China suffered the first humiliating defeat in the Opium War 1840-1842. See p. 90.

Emperor Xianfeng:

Aisin Gioro Yizhu (1851-1861). The Qing Dynasty rule was shaken by the Taiping and Nian revolutions in the south, while the Anglo-French army invaded and occupied the capital in the north. The Yuanmingyuan (Old Summer Palace) was burned down by the Anglo-French invaders. After his death, his concubine, later known as the Empress

Dowager Cixi, began her 48-year rule. See pp. 94, 98, 110, 116.

Emperor Tongzhi:

Aisin Gioro Zaichun (1862-1874). Succeeded his father, Emperor Xianfeng, at the age of six. The actual rule of the country was in the hands of his mother, Empress Dowager Cixi. See p. 122.

Emperor Guangxu:

Aisin Gioro Zaitian (1875-1908). Son of Emperor Xianfeng's younger brother and the Empress Dowager's younger sister. In the later part of his reign, unsuccessful political reform led to a national revolution against the Manchu rule and the deaths of him and the Empress Dowager, which occurred at nearly the same time, heralded the downfall of the dynasty.

Emperor Xuantong:

Aisin Gioro Puyi (1909-1911). The son of Emperor Guangxu's brother, he was designated heir-apparent of Emperor Tongzhi two days before Empress Cixi's death and one day before Emperor Guangxu's. Under his father's regency, the three-year-old boy became the last emperor of the Qing Dynasty. In the 1930s he collaborated with the Japanese and became the bogus emperor of the "Manchu Empire". As a war criminal, he was pardoned in the year 1961 and became a citizen of the People's Republic of China. See his book *From Emperor to Citizen* published by Foreign Languages Press, Beijing, China.